MW00622863

APPLY

YOUR

WISDOM

BE A GENIUS

by

LLOYD MASSIE

Copyright © 2021 by Lloyd Massie

All rights reserved in the United States.

Printed in the United States of America.

Audio Version Narrated by Matt Massie

Edited by Millie Skidmore

Cover art by Ryan Moose

Cover Editing by Dixie McGrath

This a non-fiction work.

ISBN:978-0-578-92920-0

U.S.A. Copyright: 1-10532266311

Dedication to My Greatest Teachers
I am forever thankful for:
Dan Mitchell, Linda Mitchell,
Marguerite Hightower,
John Smoker, Gary Bowe,
Jerry Webb, Charles Cox,
Elaine Perrin, Eddie Chance,
Tony Ash, Rick Marrs,
Richard Rogers, David Capers,
Rebecca Capers, Sally Caplinger,
Alok Kalia, George Willey, and
Ludy and Rose Massie.

I am so thankful for my family. The first time I saw Pamela Kai Ellis my jaw dropped. I had never seen anyone so beautiful in my entire life. I would discover that she was beautiful on the inside as well. She taught me so much over the 46 years we have been married, things like how to be compassionate, how to see the best in everyone, how to think first before acting, as well as many other lessons that are too numerous to mention. I truly married up.
We have been blessed in numerous ways. Our three children Matthew, Meredith and Neal are our greatest gifts from The Almighty.

Special thanks to Millie Skidmore for editing, Ryan Moose for cover design, Matt Massie for creating the audio version, and to the Best Math Team ever for your feedback, suggestions, and support - Trish Sierra, Korinne Stinson, Celeste Young, and Tom Collins are fabulous in every way.

TABLE OF CONTENTS

1

PREFACE

This book is written primarily in narrative form and is about my experiences and memoirs, both in and out of schools where I was either teaching or a student. It includes things I learned to do, things I intend to never do again, changes in my life, what I learned from embarrassing times and general techniques and processes I have picked up over the years I have been teaching, both borrowed from others and ones I invented on my own.

Use anything you find that might aid your teaching. Many topics covered are things I wish someone had told me were likely to happen, before they happened.

I am very thankful for all my teachers and mentors. Many thanks to them for their hard work and dedication. There are too many to talk about here, although I want to mention one, Dr. Dan Mitchell. His work teaching me the three levels of Neuro Linguistic Programming (NLP) changed my life. I am forever grateful to him.

After completing the three levels of NLP I returned to the classroom, teaching secondary math. I discovered on the first day of class that year that many things had changed during my 14 years working in other fields. I had changed more than the system had changed. Therefore, I began the process of reinventing my life in the classroom. Seems like we change more from year to year than we are aware, or not.

Continual growth is the goal. As teachers, we are lifetime learners. My hope for you is that you will stay. Many fantastic teachers I have known were so excited beginning their career.

Several said that what it was actually like to begin our profession was not anything like they envisioned. Too many left after a short time.

I believe that it takes about 5 years to learn how to do our job. In the first 5 years, you will see just about every mistake people make when learning a subject and attempt to head the mistakes off before they happen. You will figure out what the politics are in your school. You will be in just about every kind of meeting with parents and administrators. You'll find people you can trust and some you cannot. Getting stabbed in the back a few times might happen. You will become an expert in your chosen subject, as well as learning what you need to do to get your students to learn. I hope you stick with it.

I teach high school math, which is still fun, believe it or not. I also have a degree in Biblical Studies. I was in full time ministry for a decade. Being a disciple of Christ is my highest priority. Therefore, it is impossible for me to remove my spiritual life from the writing of this book. My prayer is for God's blessings on you and your work.

"Sometimes it is the people who no one imagines anything of who do the things that no one can imagine." (A line used 3 times in the movie **The Imitation Game**.) May it be true of your life.

Affirmation: I am a genius and I apply my wisdom.

2

THE DAY I DISCOVERED I HAD DECIDED I WAS WORTHLESS

During Neuro Linguistic Programming Master Practitioner Certification training, we learned a technique that elicited the values of any person. It was a tough one. It took quite a while to do. The effect also included bringing up any baggage buried in the recesses of the mind.

One of my fellow master practitioners and I decided we would practice on each other. We met up one day and began working.

The first series of questions elicited the values that were the most important to me. To get to my top 10 values she would ask which one was more important, grace or logic? She kept going until I had had to evaluate each one on the list and my top values were ranked in order from 1 to 10.

Then she started with number 1 on the list and kept asking "for what purpose?" She would say, "grace, for what purpose?" and I might say, "purity". Each value on my list of 10 kept moving up the scale as I answered "for what purpose?" at least 10 times on each one.

By the time I was down to value number 6, instead of answering for what purpose so many times I was bypassing the between answers to the question and was just going to the answer at the top. Where was each value ending? They were all ending at the same value. This proved to be quite devastating.

The value running at the top of each list was named "*worthless*". Sometime in my earliest days I had accepted the limiting belief that I was *"worthless"*. I had to face the truth. As far back as I could recall I had been believing that I was *"worthless"* and would never amount to anything.

My mind actually recalled the occasion when a lady in a blue dress had told me I was *"worthless"* and would never amount to anything. I was about 4. I had accepted her statement as the absolute truth.

Oh No!

This revelation had been hidden from my conscious mind for 37 years. What if I couldn't handle it?

It also explained many things. For example, during the course of my life, any time I came close to success, I would self-destruct because I believed I was supposed to be *"worthless"*.

For example, one day in basketball practice my junior year we had a scrimmage. Afterwards my coach asked me if I knew how many shots I had made. I had no idea. He said that I had shot 18 of 19 from the field and wondered why I never did that in a real game. Scrimmages during practice didn't really count. I might self-destruct in a real game because I believed I was *"worthless"*.

What an epiphany! I was blown away. My mind was spinning. I felt like throwing up. What could be done about this limiting belief I had accepted as the truth?

My friend said I could change the limiting belief if I wanted to. I did. She had me imagine going backwards on the timeline of my life searching for the first event where the limiting belief *"worthless"* was born. I closed my eyes and imagined going down my timeline off into my past. It took some time to get to the right spot. I had to stay very high above my timeline to avoid falling apart.

She asked me to back up about 10 minutes before the event where I decided I was *"worthless"* was about to happen. I did. Then she told me to release all negative emotions and limiting decisions in the event that was about to happen, letting them float up above the timeline and make their way into the sun where they would be burned up and totally destroyed forever.

This took a while. I had a visual that looked like an explosion of confetti shooting out of my timeline. *"Worthless"* was finally all gone. Then she had me move forward and jump into the spot on the timeline where the event had been. She said look around, see what you see, feel what you feel, etc. *"Worthless"* was gone. One limiting decision made way in the past had been controlling my life for 37 years.

She had me turn and look towards the present time and move slowly along my timeline allowing everything to change and adjust until I got back to the present. Then she sent me out onto my future timeline a few months to see how I was getting along. I felt great when I jumped onto my timeline a few months in the future.

It was scary to change the way I had always been. Just what was life going to be like now? She said my wife might leave me (she didn't), as I was not the same person she had married.

Driving home that day was a feeling of complete exhilaration. I had gone from finding out I thought I was *"worthless"* and feeling as low as the floor, to freedom. It was a great day. I hadn't been home 10 minutes when my wife commented that she didn't know who I was, as I had changed my personality. I said I was the same old me without all my negative baggage.

After I spoke at church the next Sunday, as I was a minister at the time, I was feeling fantastic. I was free from the prison my limiting decision had created. The church board knew something had changed, too. I was no longer the man they had hired. In the end, they did not deal with my changes very well. I chalked it up to the price of change.

Monday came and I went to the Kiwanis luncheon downtown. Afterward, I was visiting with the two women that run the place who were members of our church. Mary pulled me aside and asked me what I had done. Something was different on Sunday, she said. She said as I was speaking on Sunday that there was a thick blue halo all around me. Really? That was news to me. A blue halo? No one else mentioned it.

My freedom event happened in 1994. I have been living in a different world since then. It is more fun. It still has problems, but it is more fun. I have been blackballed some over the years, as some people have not known how to react to a man that is what they call, *extremely confident.*

Since the only thing I can control is myself, I just let it go and go about doing what is the next best thing in all areas of my life. My wish for all of you is that you would release any decision that has placed limits on yourself, as well as all unresolved negative emotions that have been stored over the course of your life.

Perhaps your unconscious mind, with your permission of course, could just go clean up your timeline for you, tonight while you are sleeping. There might also be an NLP Master Practitioner in your neighborhood that could help you, if you really want to find the underlying cause of what is actually going on.

My suggestion is to find a place teaching NLP Practitioner and NLP Master Practitioner and take them, whatever the cost. It might be the best thing that you could do for you. I know it was for me. The only downside is facing your own baggage, which didn't make me feel good, and wound up disappearing forever.

Then after Master Practitioner, if you are brave enough, take on NLP Trainer Training. Wow! Learning how to teach the unconscious mind is wild and a huge stretch that is well worth the effort. It will help you make tons of progress. Have fun!

Affirmation: I am a genius and I apply my wisdom.

3

CAUSE AND EFFECT

Cause is greater than effect.

Either you live *at cause*, or you live at effect.

Either you accept responsibility for what is happening in your life, or you blame someone else.

When *at cause* you will overcome every obstacle in your way.

When at effect you might whine about how awful your situation is.

When *at cause* you will find the way through.

When at effect you can get stuck and see no way through.

When *at cause* you most often make good decisions.

When at effect, most often you make no decisions or poor ones.

When *at cause* you have a prepared plan for every possible event.

When at effect most calamities give you another opportunity to say how awful it all is.

When *at cause* you will be successful at what you are doing because you expect to be.

When at effect you will not be successful because you expect not to be.

When *at cause* people like to be around you.

When at effect not as many people want to be around you.

When *at cause* some drama is a show you watch on television.

When at effect some drama is what you might be creating.

When *at cause* you make the students pass their State Assessment Test.

When at effect your students do not pass their State Assessment Test because you don't have advanced students.

When *at cause* you believe criticism about you is just feedback.

When at effect you might believe the criticism to be true.

When *at cause* you have a face to face meeting with your antagonist.

When at effect you might stab your antagonist in the back.

When *at cause* you win an argument because you are right.

When at effect you demonize your opponent because your own argument is lame.

When *at cause* you bloom where you are planted.

When at effect you are always trying to leave and work somewhere else.

When *at cause* your confidence is usually high.

When at effect you might say you lost your confidence.

When *at cause* you easily discard any process or technique that is no longer successful.

When at effect you keep doing what has ceased to work, you just do it harder.

When *at cause* you make an A from the worst professor at your college.

When at effect you justify your lower grade because the professor is so bad.

When *at cause* you handle money wisely.

When at effect you might spend every dime you have.

When *at cause* you have a plan that you follow through.

When at effect you make a plan and might procrastinate.

When *at cause* you might own the company.

When at effect you could be passed over for promotions.

When *at cause* you have lots of respect.

When at effect your respect quotient is lower.

When *at cause* you might retire early.

When at effect you might not be able to retire.

When *at cause* you might retire from one job, do another one, retire from it, and wind up with multiple retirements.

When at effect you might work just as many years for one retirement.

When *at cause* if your students don't understand something, you explain it to them again until they get it.

When at effect if your students don't understand something, you say that they are just whiners.

When *at cause* you solve your own student problems with their parents.

When at effect it is the principals fault the problem is not solved.

When *at cause* you are not worried about getting your teacher contract for the next school year.

When at effect you might worry that you will not get a contract for next year and for good reason.

When *at cause* you are dressed and groomed appropriately.

When at effect you might look slouchy.

Surely, by now you get the point.

I freely admit that I have lived *at cause* and I have lived at effect, sometimes during the same week. There have also been times when I was stuck living at effect.

All I know is living *at cause* is more fun. I am making more money, having more fun and am getting more respect than at any single point in my life.

Live *at cause* and you will live in a new world.

Your new world will still have problems.

You will just handle them head on *at cause*.

You will be glad you did.

Affirmation: I am a genius and I apply my wisdom.

4

RAPPORT ON THE UNCONSCIOUS LEVEL

Rapport is a very powerful tool. When you have rapport, your students will track with everything you do, as well as do everything you ask them to do. The need to write discipline referrals will be low, or there might not even be any. Your classroom management will appear to be perfect, as reflected in your annual evaluation.

As classroom teachers, we all know that rapport is a tremendous asset. We wish we had a higher level of rapport with students, parents, administrators, administrative assistants, registrars, janitors, counselors and colleagues. We know the peace that comes as well as any help when we need it, when our rapport is strong with the people that work in our building.

Unfortunately, the opposite is true as well. Disconnections with people at any level have caused many turf wars in your average school. Too often, to get ahead, others have pushed their colleagues down. To me this is sad since it can be avoided, if rapport on the unconscious level was learned and practiced.

Rapport on the unconscious level is all about reducing the differences between you and another person as close to zero as possible. We know that we have a serious deep connection with our inner circle. At times, our inner circle will know we are struggling and will call to see what's up. You may get calls from all over your city, state, or country, as the people you are connected with the strongest will sense that they need to call you, as something just seems out of balance. You call them, too, when your unconscious prompts you to do so. The connection is very deep. What has made it so deep is unconscious rapport.

So once upon a time, I went to NLP Practitioner training one day, eager to see what Dr. Dan had for us to learn and experience. Turned out it was building unconscious rapport day. He talked about building unconscious rapport for a while as he set up our first exercise.

I found myself in a group of 3 other practitioners as we got ready to build unconscious rapport with one another. Three roles would be played during the exercise, the Speaker, the Listener and the Observer.

The speaker was to tell a story about either their favorite vacation, or make up a story about their dream vacation. The listener was to build unconscious rapport with the speaker using all the techniques Dr. Dan had taught us. The observer was to closely watch and monitor the listener to see if they were really listening. Three rounds later, everyone had the experience of all three roles.

Carol was the first speaker in my group. I was the first listener. I did not like her very much, as she had been making comments during the course that were turning me off. I had tried to get in another group, but Dr. Dan assigned me there and said Carol was to speak first and I was to build rapport with her. He knew. I'm not sure just how he knew, but he knew. I was thinking about going home when Carol began to talk about her vacation.

All righty then, so away we went. I began tracking with her during her story, doing my best to practice all the prescribed techniques correctly. About two minutes into her story, we were behaving like *"best friends forever !"* I felt as if I had known her my entire life and that we had some long strong deep connection with each other. When I glanced at Dr. Dan he put his thumbs up.

This experience blew me away. I could hardly believe that I had changed from being annoyed to death by this lady, to feeling like she was my best friend on the planet, in less than two minutes. We did not stop talking to each other when Dr. Dan was ready to continue, as he had to ask us to stop. This change was shocking.

To reduce the difference between two people to as near zero as possible, here is what he instructed us to do, in no certain order, as we were to do all of these simultaneously.

: Sit with the same posture as the speaker, including the folding of hands, position of their feet, tilt of the head, etc. Copy their sitting position exactly. Copy all movements of hands, legs, feet, head, etc. Stay focused on matching everything.

: Make comments of short semi-repeats of parts of their story, using all their predicates. Matching their verbs was a big deal. Carol is visual (she was using all visual verbs), I am auditory. I had to speak using visual verbs, which would match with her primary representational system, adapting myself to the language of her world.

: Blink when she blinked.

: Breathe at the same rate and pace as she was.

:Recount a similar experience, like, "Oh that same thing happened to me!" Keep comments real short, so she could continue on with her vacation story.

:Watch for any signs that unconscious rapport has been reached. I saw a lightning quick blush go across her left check and almost as instantly disappear. I was looking for some sign on her face and had I not been so focused I would have missed the quick blush.

: I felt the unconscious rapport as well in the middle of my chest. This was the first time I had ever had a kinesthetic response in any of our exercises. While

16

writing this today, 20 years later, I get the same kinesthetic feeling in my chest. Actually my unconscious mind has learned to alert me with this trigger as a signal that unconscious rapport has been reached.

I have been practicing building unconscious rapport since 1994. In the beginning, I was overtly copying all their physiology. I found that this was excessively uncomfortable for me. Therefore, I stopped all the matching and just focused on intense listening, repeating short quips in their primary representational system. I listen intently to their predicates, asking myself in wonderment what the world that they live in must be like.

What has to be true in another person's model of the world for me to be hearing and seeing what I am hearing and seeing? What is the world they are living in really like? Ask yourself these questions about every student you teach.

I get two pieces of feedback that tell me I have established unconscious rapport. I will see the expression on their face and feel it as I get the kinesthetic trigger in my chest. During a normal school day the rapport building is continuous. It keeps going and going and going. Everything that happens or does not happen is just one more opportunity to build some more unconscious rapport.

The students write me notes sometimes, mostly towards the end of the year and they will say things like: "No one ever talked to me the way you talk to me!" "I am so glad I took your class this year, I will always remember you." It is true that I love them. They know it, without me having to mention it.

UPDATE: Last year I had a surgery and missed 7 days of school around the Thanksgiving break. There was a stack of notes from my students on my desk when I returned. Most said how much they missed me being at school. Two offered to donate a kidney, if I needed one. I didn't need one, but was blown away by the offer. Rapport is a very powerful tool.

I have also learned that the rapport is ongoing with all of them. I have taught 19 years in Round Rock and have averaged about 150 students per year, or about 2,550 students. I bump into them all over town, almost everywhere I go. "Mr. Massie do you remember me?" they usually ask. I remember all their faces. I need a new strategy for their names, as too often I have to ask them. The internal rapport begins to fire off, as it is still present for my ex-students as well as myself.

Affirmation: I am a genius and I apply my wisdom.

5

EMBARRASSED AT THE SALT GRASS

Nine years ago when our first grandson was born, my wife texted me to come over to our daughters after work and that I should eat on the way as they had already eaten dinner. This slight change in plans was okay, as I had been hanging out at our house waiting for my wife to return, so we could go over to play with the baby.

All right, it is Friday night, 7 pm, and I am deciding just where to stop and eat. I picked The Salt Grass, which is a great steak place, and wondered when I parked if I was in for a long wait. I checked the bar and there was a single seat left. I took it and ordered a New York strip steak without looking at the menu. The waiter brought me an iced tea and life was good.

It was very loud in the bar. The noise was due to about 20 women whom I suspected were all together and waiting for a large table. They were talking it up during happy hour.

The waiter brought my New York Strip steak. When he sat it down the girl sitting next to me turned around and said "Oh, that looks good!" I said "Thanks". Our eyes locked and she shouted, "Mr. Massie!!!" and she gave me a big hug. I was then introduced to her 2 grandmothers, her mother, and about a dozen or more siblings and cousins.

Away she went describing to them how she would not have graduated high school if I had not been her math teacher. I had not seen her in 5 years. She had gotten a bachelor's degree at The University of Texas at Austin and was working, in what she called, her first real job. She was all grown up and looked fabulous. Our rapport was just as deep 5 years in the future.

However, I have to tell the truth about that experience. I could not remember her name, which was embarrassing. Too many names and 5 years removed. I finally gave up the charade and asked. She chided me with, "Mr. Massie, I had you 3 years in a row!" This got a big laugh from all her relatives.

I may never see her again, but still feel a strong connection, as we know each other on an unconscious level.

Like all my ex-students, I am very proud of her. She overcame any and all obstacles in high school and college, completed her work, and is off making something productive out of her life. As I recall, math was not her favorite subject. Go figure. It was my pleasure to work with her. She made lots of progress mathematically while in my classes, which is always my goal. Leave them upstream from where they are when they walk in the door.

How fun is the career we have in teaching, right? We are seeking to make a difference in the life of another human being that just happens to be a teenager. Another former student sent me a note that says, "Now every time I have a decision to make, I first ask myself, what would Massie think?" That one cracked me up. The thought that she would even care what I thought is just one more piece of feedback that says, unconscious rapport is a very powerful tool.

Achieving unconscious rapport is really a trip. It takes lots of effort. You have to learn to pay attention to everything. What is the look on their face? What verbs are they using? Have they let you in yet? Any idea what is holding them back?

I do most all my unconscious rapport building in one on one conversations. What message is the look on their face sending me? In the beginning their look says, "Can I really trust you?" Once they have decided that they can, they tend to look me in the eye, and I feel the rapport that has been built.

They know when we care about them and when we don't! Would you trust somebody that you thought didn't care about you? If you thought that your teacher didn't like teenagers, how much respect would you have for them? Looking back to your high school years, which teachers did you trust? Why did you trust them? Which teacher had the biggest impact on your life? How did they do it? The chances are high that you still feel a connection with them, because unconscious rapport is very powerful.

So it's time to go off building unconscious rapport with everyone you meet. I promise that you will have many occasions to practice unconscious rapport building. You could always practice in a group of 3, if you wanted too, or not. As always you get to decide. Have fun!

Affirmation: I am a genius and I apply my wisdom.

6

A GREATEST HOUR

One year I decided to change the way I attended graduation. My reason was that I always wanted to talk to all of my students, most of whom were seniors, but hardly, if ever, saw any of them after graduation.

When there are 800 in a graduating class and a crowd of 7,000 people, it was not all that surprising that I couldn't find any of them afterwards as they were all taking pictures with their families and friends.

So, I decided to make sure I went to pre-graduation. I did not sign up to be a line leader, but just showed up an hour early. They had the graduates all standing in rows like cord wood down under the stands backstage.

I went up and down each row looking for my 100 plus seniors. It was an awesome hour as I talked to all of them, took pictures, commented that I had never seen them so dressed up, etc. What a blast!

When graduation began I had already achieved what I had set out to do that day, which was see some of them for the last time, more than likely.

On that occasion, they are so excited and anxious to walk across the stage. Some of them could hardly believe that I had come looking for them.

I resolved to go to pre-graduation until I retired. Those hours are some of the most memorable and precious to me. There was always lots of hugs, smiles and laughs.

Affirmation: I am a genius and I apply my wisdom.

7

THE GUY AT WELLS FARGO

I went into the bank one day and was making a deposit when the man at the next space said hello. He asked me if I remembered him. His face looked familiar. I asked if I had taught him in school. "Yes", he said. He then apologized for being such a jerk and causing me so much trouble when he was in school. Ok.

I had no recall of anything he might have done when he was a teenager. He felt some remorse for past behaviors. It was important to him to apologize to me. We visited for a while. He told me what he had been up to during the 10 years that had passed since he was in high school. He was really doing well.

Two things we all need to do are:
1. Make amends for any of our past wrongs. Getting it off our chest, so to speak, clearing the deck, saying we are sorry for unruly behavior, doing whatever it takes to apologize will help us move forward. Write a few letters, make a few calls or send some texts or messages. Whatever it takes.
2. Since we all made lots of mistakes along the road, give your former students a break. They are not like they were in high school. They have grown out of a lot of their irresponsibility. They most likely have some level of guilt for trouble they might have caused in school.

We want all of our students to grow up and become productive adults in the real world. Some do it faster than others. They all learn. We know that we all have an internal file cabinet that might be titled, "Things I'll will never do again." It is full of things we tried that did not work out so well.

Another guy, Mr. Wilson was a real pill in my class. For some reason I remember him acting out, unlike the guy I bumped into in Wells Fargo. And yes, I bumped into Mr. Wilson, too. I had just finished putting gas in my car, when the truck on the opposite side of the pump pulled up a little bit and rolled down the window.

"Mr. Massie?" he said. "Wilson?" I said. He had been out of high school for 5 years, had become a Marine, finished his 4 years of service and was taking Calculus 2 at the local community college. He had almost failed Algebra 2 when he was in my class.

He apologized for being a jerk. I pretended I didn't remember. We talked for a while. He told me his goal was to finish an engineering degree at Texas A & M. He had grown up. The Marines had been great for him. I remember thinking that he was very smart, but just goofing off and not really bringing it.

He figured it out. Good for him. I bet he is making a great engineer.

Makes we wonder how all my other former students are doing?

Affirmation: I am a genius and I apply my wisdom.

8

THE SCREAMING TRANSFER

One year, two weeks before the end of the fall semester, Miss O was transferred into my Algebra 2 class. She had a 50 average. What was up? Why now? Would I be fussed at because my failure rate was too high due to this change?

I had a negative reaction to this transfer, fussed at Miss O when she showed me her admit slip, and got very grouchy.

When the last period of the day ended, I headed to the office, intending to talk with Miss O's counselor and find out what happened. When I met the counselor in the hall, she promptly stopped and said she knew I would be looking for her, but that it was not her call. She was told to move Miss O into my class.

So, what's going on? She told me that I needed to go see Mr. P. When I walked into his office, he said, "Come on in, I was expecting you."

I told him that it made no sense whatsoever to move a student two weeks before the end of a semester. Just leaving her where she was and moving her at the break made more sense.

He told me that there had been a meeting in the conference room with Miss O, her mother, her counselor, her Algebra 2 teacher, our campus principal and himself and that it had gotten ugly. The mom and the Algebra 2 teacher were both standing and screaming at each other across the conference table.

After everyone had gone except the administrators, the campus principal had said to move her as soon as possible.

Mr. P then said that it was a compliment to me. I told him that I didn't feel complimented. Sending me an unruly and failing student whose mother had been screaming in a meeting did not sound like a compliment to me.

The campus principal had asked which Algebra 2 teacher would be the best place to move Miss O? Mr. P said that he heard all kinds of complaints about everyone teaching Algebra 2, but had never heard one about me. He told the principal that Mr. Massie would diffuse this situation.

Ugh! Thanks a lot.

They were now expecting me to handle Miss O, deal with her mother, eliminate all the issues that had created the big argument and get her grade to passing. Oh boy, thanks guys! How much trouble was Miss O about to cause?

She never caused any trouble at all, I never talked to her mother and she made straight A's during the second semester. She was a very sweet girl. This was the opposite of what I feared was going to happen. Hmm........ Reminds me of the line that was used twice in the movie Seabiscuit, "You don't throw a whole life away, just because it's banged up a little bit." Sometimes all we need is a second chance.

Miss O had a very high math aptitude and was an A student with a 50 average when she was transferred into my classroom. She joined our class and was an asset to everything I was trying to get done. I never had to call her down as her behavior was perfect.

In the end, the problem was really with the other Algebra 2 teacher and Miss O's mom. Miss O and her mother had a huge clash with my colleague and they had gone to war, so to speak. In my class things were so smooth that I never heard from Miss O's mother.

The administrators never mentioned it either. Neither did the other Algebra 2 teacher. Why were all the other Algebra 2 teachers getting complaints? I have no clue.

Could it be the case that many students, in the average high school, develop such an intense dislike for a teacher that they would rather just go to war, even if they fail the course? Perhaps.

Seems like situations like this are really just one more opportunity to go build some rapport. As I recall, I did not go out of my way dealing with Miss O, but just went about my daily routine, like always.

The first few weeks I kept a close eye on her, reading what I could. She was holding back, processing if she was going to be able to trust me, or not? Would I be just like the teacher before, or not? Was she about to re-experience the same thing again and wind up in a meeting with her mother screaming at me?

She caved pretty quickly. I never talked to her about any of this. Once she trusted me everything was smooth sailing. That's right, we can all tell when someone trusts us.

I don't like conflict. Who does? Getting along works better. Do whatever you can to get both student and parent on the same side of doing whatever it takes to make learning happen. You'll have more fun.

Because of Miss O I now ask each class every year if any of their teachers hate them? Oh Boy! They sure think that some of us do! I also ask if you hate any of your teachers. Ouch! Sometimes I have to stop them from naming names.

Build as much rapport as you can. Your conflicts will be less. You will have more fun. Your students will do better. There you go.

Affirmation: I am a genius and I apply my wisdom.

9

ATTACHED

Miss Griffith was a student in my Advanced Placement Statistics class the first year I taught AP Statistics. I had never taught the class before and had not taken Statistics in college. I knew I would have my work cut out for me, teaching it to myself. Most of that first year teaching AP Statistics is a blur, but I can remember studying the material very hard.

I would not have caught up on all the various graphing calculator functions as fast as I did, had it not been for Miss Griffith. Her brilliance was obvious from the start. She processed things so quickly all she needed was to see it once, and she could remember it, do the process, and teach anyone who was not up to speed.

I have only ever had the privilege of teaching what I would call, 2 genius level instant learners. Beth Jennings was the best student I had ever seen, until Miss Griffith came along. They would both listen to the lesson while they were doing every problem on a particular page, reasoning that it wouldn't matter which problems I was going to assign, since they had already done the whole page. They could listen to the first little bit of the lesson and their brains would finish all the other aspects of a topic, because to them the rest was just a logical foregone conclusion.

I got attached to Miss Griffith pretty fast. I know what you're thinking. We are not supposed to get so attached to students, as we are to treat everyone equally, and never be friends with them, keeping our distance between teacher and student on a professional level, etc. You are right! I got attached anyway.

The truth is that some students we just get to know better. Maybe it is because they are more extroverted, or we just interact with them more as they come for help more often, or our personalities are more like theirs and we just know them better. Maybe our internal filters are similar.

Not all students will let us in, either. The wall can be hard to get through, at times. They are keeping their distance as well.

I love all my students, for sure, but some are easier to love and you are just going to love some of them more. They have teachers that they love more as well. Every year I ask if any of their teachers hate them and it is not hard to get them talking about that topic. They grade us on our teaching abilities and judging by these grades you would be both the best teacher they ever had in their entire life or the worst one.

The end of the year came and during a test Miss Griffith asked me if I would sign her Yearbook. I said okay and went into stall mode.

I have taught over 2,500 students the past 21 years in the town where I teach. Most of them I will never see again. Some of them I know better than others. My wife and I will bump into ex-students from time to time when we are out eating or shopping. I will never see all 2,500 of them again.

I became overwhelmed with the thought that I might never see Miss Griffith again and was having a hard time even thinking about signing her yearbook. She naturally finished her test first, with a perfect paper, again, and asked me if I had signed her Yearbook, yet. I said no but that I would get right on it. She commented 10 minutes later that I still hadn't signed it.

So, I picked it up and began. "Would I ever see her again?" kept running through my mind. I began to write. I turned my back to the class as my emotions got the best of me. I was overwhelmed. I would write a while and cry awhile. In the end, I had written an entire page in her yearbook.

Love is the most powerful force. Separated from my son who had passed from this life 2 years prior, the thought of losing touch with Miss Griffith had pushed me over the edge. I have a tremendous fear of loss. It is an extremely real fear. Would I ever see her again? What had happened to make me feel and behave as if she was one of my own children?

Towards the end of the period, I regained my composer and turned back around. A number of students who saw what was going on had busted me. They were giving me some interesting looks. She picked up her yearbook when the period ended and said she would see me next time.

She wrote me a letter and brought it to the next class meeting. That summer I had the letter framed and it hangs on the wall behind my desk. I want to see it there every day, as a reminder to myself that I have a very important job and to remember Miss Griffith.

I am privileged to work with high school students, to love them as I do my own, to encourage them as best I can, to give life building skills, to share my values and maybe even teach them some mathematics. My influence they will remember, whereas just some of the math they will remember.

When I see her letter each day, I remember that my job goes way beyond the teaching of mathematics.

Miss Griffith has now graduated from college and is a high school chemistry teacher. We have kept in touch. She calls from time to time. I used to text her to see how her college work was going. My wife is attached to her too, along with our daughter and grandsons.

We have tons of opportunities to change the world by influencing the next generation of high school kids. Sharing your life is always a great choice. All your kids at your school will appreciate all the unconditional love you share. It will make a big difference in their lives.

Look back and be amazed at all that has occurred during your journey of teaching.

Affirmation: I am a genius and I apply my wisdom.

10

PATTERN INTERRUPT

People run patterns. They work well due to practice and years of use. Patterns are repeated, sometimes every day. Some patterns are positive, some are not. Some patterns can be hard to break. Some can be easy to break. Some patterns are liabilities. Some patterns are assets.

If you have ever tried to change something about yourself and noticed that you wound up going back to square one and starting all over, the chances are high that your old pattern pulled you back. Some students of mine have tried to stop biting their nails and did well, until they were stressed at school and started biting them again. They are finding it hard to stop biting their nails, so they say. Patterns are powerful and have a tendency to pull us back when we are trying to change them. Even with a minor problem like nail biting, the pattern can pull you back.

So what are we to do about all of our minor problems, or our major ones for that matter?

PATTERN INTERRUPT is one thing you can do. Just interrupt the pattern. Interrupt it until it breaks and cannot work anymore. Once it is broken, you will want to replace it with a new pattern that is more to your liking. Make sure you pick a good one to replace the one you changed.

The PATTERN INTERRUPT experts say that the magic numbers are 3 and 21. What they mean is that if the undesired pattern is interrupted somewhere between 3 and 21 times it will be broken, and stop running. It cannot run any more, which is good, since you wanted to change it anyway. So if the nail bitter stopped the biting of their nails the next 21 times they were stressed the old nail biting pattern would stop.

If the new pattern is "chicken fried steak" when stressed, then at the very least, what it would mean is that their nails would look great.

Okay, so the goal is to interrupt an undesirable pattern. Sounds easy enough. It well may be easy all right, or not.

As I was reinventing my teaching career, it was only natural for me to want to help my students break all old patterns of not success. As you know if you teach math, we deal with multiple old patterns of not success with lots of our students. Many have not enjoyed success in prior math classes and of all the subjects taught in school, math might be the one that is their least favorite. Okay, I will just say it, some of them do not like math.

"Has math always been your favorite subject?" I ask every student this question at some point each year, just to see what they say. I hear all kinds of interesting answers.

Therefore, this is a very challenging assignment. I need to take a room full of high school students that may not all like math, may have not been successful at math, have years of old negative patterns regarding math, and find a way to do PATTERN INTERRUPT with their old patterns, while I am making math fun. Sounds like an opportunity. I decided to give it a shot. What old patterns could I interrupt and just where did I want to begin.

What is often the case in everyone's favorite class, Algebra, is that they have this old pattern that says they can't do math, so the old pattern helps them do all the not correct rules, because after all they are not supposed to get anything right, so the pattern helps them do it not right. From my viewpoint they just don't have the rules down.

To illustrate this I will pick an Algebra topic, so let us pick signed numbers, specifically the adding and subtracting of all combinations of positive and negative numbers. If you do not know how to correctly apply the rules about the negative sign you are guaranteed to get lots of problems not correct. It was a good place to start.

The rules are easy for addition and subtraction. Math teachers bear with me as there may be teachers reading this that teach other subjects. Anyway, "if the signs of the two numbers are the same you add the numbers and keep the sign." "If the signs of the two numbers are different you subtract the numbers and keep the sign of the bigger number." Those are the two rules for addition and subtraction of a pair of signed numbers.

A fair majority of all mistakes in Algebra happen around a negative sign. Once a student quits making mistakes with their negative signs their grade can go up fast.

Therefore, I looked for a way to do PATTERN INTERRUPT for any student who did not have these rules mastered. Whatever I came up with would need to include at the very least 21 repetitions of success. So how could I get the whole room to complete 21 examples of success with their negative signs?

Here is what I did. I brought 15 decks of cards to class. The class was excited to see decks of cards laying out and immediately assumed that there was at least a possibility they might have fun in math class today.

The activity I used was one I learned from my good friend and master teacher Mike Tucker. Thanks Mike. Mike's game goes something like this.

Black cards are positive and red cards are negative. Jacks count 11, queens 12, and kings 13, aces 1, and all other cards their number. You will be playing against a classmate, so each player turns a card face up after the cards are dealt evenly and face down, the first player to play, looks at the cards and if they are the same color adds and keeps the sign, if they are different colors subtracts and uses the sign of the bigger number. If they get the correct answer, they get to keep both cards. If they do not, they lose the cards to their opponent. Back and forth, they play until round one is finished. (About 7 minutes) The winner is the player with the most cards. Then I have the kids switch and play against another student. Each player's won/loss record is recorded on the board. The kids really like this activity.

I like the game for lots of reasons including the practice of signed numbers, and for the fact that they were doing the adding and subtracting in their head. I did not ban calculators for this game, but no one asked if they could use one, which was good. Actually, it did not dawn on me until later that the game had been calculator free.

I walked around the room watching. The kids were actually having fun and as time passed, there were fewer and fewer wrong answers.

If the pattern you want to interrupt is a misapplication of the rules, then by the time the class period was over that old pattern is over too. There were many more correct answers than 21. There was plenty of evidence the kids had mastered the addition and subtraction of signed numbers. The won loss record was on the board.

After signed numbers,as the days passed, I went after the distributive property, solving first and second degree equations, and so on with every topic in the curriculum.

If your old pattern was "I don't like math", that pattern was interrupted only one day. Only 20 more days to "like math" to go. The good thing of course is I have 175 days each year to break the "I don't like math" pattern.

Each school day I am on the lookout for patterns that need interrupting. If they say, "I'm about to fail this test!" Then I say, "I know!" Then they say, "Do you want me to fail!" Then

I say, "No, I want you to pass the test, but you already decided that you were not passing it, so it is totally out of my control".

Then they say, "Well then maybe I will change my mind and pass the test." Then I say, "That's better."

I just interrupted a pattern once. Maybe their confidence was shaky or maybe they just wanted me to give them some attention, or maybe there is no way to tell what they were doing. All I know is that in order to make the most of every opportunity, I have resolved to use every opportunity to coach the students towards excellence.

The challenge for you as a classroom teacher is to invent as many ways as you can to interrupt patterns you see that the kids are running that are holding them back.

Just this week the teacher next door asked me after school what he could do with his Algebra 1 class that was in his words, out of control. I made a few suggestions. He resolved to have the kids do between 20 and 30 problems in class each day and set his lesson planning in that direction. On Friday, he was excited to report that they had done 28 in class that afternoon.

Somewhere between 3 and 21 days of that level of work, the old pattern of sitting there and doing nothing is dead. It does make me wonder though, why at times, we have all allowed them to sit in class and do nothing. Find as many ways as you can to make them work.

When we do not interrupt the do nothing pattern, we feed their laziness pattern. When we make them work, we help to install a work ethic pattern that could see them through college and beyond. So make them work.

How many problems could I get a student to do in a 90-minute class period? I shoot for between 20 and 30. Sometimes I make it and sometimes I do not. I know what you are thinking. You are wondering what it is that I do, exactly. Okay here are my two favorite procedures.

1. Lecture short work long. This is easier to do in an Algebra class than in Geometry. I turn to the assignment, and look at the first section of problems. Most of the time it is somewhere between 1 to 8 problems. I do two of them on the board as examples and then tell them that part of their homework is to do the other 6 and that I want them to do them in about 2 songs. I turn on some music that I like and walk around the room watching them work. It becomes hard for them to hide if they are doing nothing when I am standing there watching them. When they are finished with section 1, repeat the process with each section until class is over. Most days I can get them to do at least 20 problems.

2. Going to the Big Board. I mark off 8 spaces on both big boards in my room, so I can send 16 students to the big boards at the same time. The other students have little white boards to use at their desks. Then everyone works the same problem at the same time and I watch and coach. Standing behind them as they work on the big board is educational. You can tell instantly who has it and who does not. So I help the strugglers and when people start finishing I have them help any who are stuck or struggling. And most of the time, the students help each other without me asking them to. The audience group holds up their boards and I provide positive feedback when they have it right, and coach them through any mistakes. When everyone is finished with the problem, I take a thumb vote and answer any questions. (Thumb up says I've got it, thumb sideways says something isn't clear, thumbs down says I'm lost.) Then we switch groups, only if all thumbs are up, and the audience from problem #1 goes to the big board.

I must ask as this chapter ends, which patterns of your own do you want to interrupt and just how will you plan to do that?

Affirmation: I am a genius and I apply my wisdom.

11

MISS YANEZ MAKES AN *A*

Miss Yanez: "I'm gonna flunk Algebra 2!"

Mr. Massie: "I know!"

Miss Yanez: "It's the first day of the school, how could you know?"

Mr. Massie: "You already decided to flunk, not sure how I could ever change your mind!"

Miss Yanez: "I hate Algebra!"

Mr. Massie: "How do you do that?"

Miss Yanez: "Do what?"

Mr. Massie: "How do you do that?"

Miss Yanez: "You mean, hate Algebra?"

Mr. Massie: "Yes, how do you do that?"

Miss Yanez: "I don't want to talk about it!"

Mr. Massie: "You brought it up; I thought you wanted to talk about it!"

Miss Yanez: "Leave me alone."

Mr. Massie: "Okay I'll leave you alone, but isn't it my job to teach you Algebra 2?"

Miss Yanez: "It's too late, I know I'm gonna flunk Algebra 2!"

Mr. Massie: "If you were to know, how do you know you're gonna flunk Algebra 2!"

Miss Yanez: "I have always flunked my math class!"

Mr. Massie: "Really? What if you could break the pattern and make an *A*?"

Miss Yanez (laughing): "Right, whatever!"

Scene Shifts to week 3 after the first Test.

Miss Yanez: "I told you!"

Mr. Massie: "You told me what?"

Miss Yanez: "That I was gonna flunk! I made a 35 on the first Test!"

Mr. Massie: "Did you get what you expected?"

Miss Yanez: "Yes, I knew I was gonna flunk!"

Mr. Massie: "You don't know the rules about the negative sign!"

Miss Yanez: "Yes I do!"

Mr. Massie: "Come up here, I want you to make something!"

Miss Yanez: "What?"

Mr. Massie: "Come on, up here at the conference table!"

Miss Yanez: "Okay, what do you want me to do?"

Mr. Massie: "On chart 1 make a heading that says, *ADDITION AND SUBTRACTION OF SIGNED NUMBERS*, in black!"

Miss Yanez: "Got it!"

Mr. Massie: Now write this question, "*ARE THE SIGNS THE SAME?*"

Miss Yanez: "*ARE THE SIGNS THE SAME?* What color do you want?"

Mr. Massie: "Use green for GO!"

Miss Yanez: "That's dorky!"

Mr. Massie: "I know, use green anyway!"

Miss Yanez: "Okay, there you go!, Now what?"

Mr. Massie: "In blue write, *IF YES, ADD AND KEEP THE SIGN!*"

Miss Yanez: "*IF YES, ADD AND KEEP THE SIGN*, okay got it!"

Mr. Massie: Now write, "*IF NO, SUBTRACT AND USE THE SIGN OF THE BIGGEST!*, in red."

Miss Yanez: "Red's my favorite color! Okay, there you go!"

Mr. Massie: "Good! Now for the 2nd chart make the heading read, *MULTIPLICATION AND DIVISION OF SIGNED NUMBERS!*"

Miss Yanez: "In black?"

Mr Massie: "Yes!"

Miss Yanez: "Okay, there you go!"

Mr. Massie: "Now in green write, *HOW MANY NEGATIVE SIGNS DO I SEE?*"

Miss Yanez: "Got it!"

Mr. Massie: "Make two columns under the heading, label the first one *EVEN NUMBER* written in blue, and the second one, *ODD NUMBER* written in red."

Miss Yanez: "I feel like I'm back in the 4th grade."

Mr. Massie: "Me too!"

Miss Yanez: "You do?"

Mr. Massie: "Of course, I'm ready to go to recess or lunch, my two favorite classes!"

Miss Yanez: "You're messing with me!"

Mr. Massie: "Under the blue one write, *THE ANSWER IS POSITIVE*! And under the red one write, *THE ANSWER IS NEGATIVE!*"

Miss Yanez: "Are we almost through?"

Mr. Massie: "All we have to do is hang them up by your new desk!"

Miss Yanez: "I have a new desk?"

Mr. Massie: "You're special!"

Miss Yanez: "I have to sit in the front by the wall?"

Mr. Massie: "Yes, right beside your new charts!"

I taped the charts on the wall beside her new desk. From then on whenever she got stuck on a sign and asked a question, as well as after the next test, I would say, go to chart one and ask the question, *ARE THE SIGNS THE SAME*? Yes or no, which one is it? Is the answer positive or negative? Or,

HOW MANY NEGATIVE SIGNS DO YOU SEE? An even number of negative signs is positive; an odd number of negative signs is negative.

She made an A on the 3rd Test, and every Test and assignment thereafter. Her mother made sure she got in my Pre-Cal class the next year. She made an *A* every grading period the next year, too. Her only issue was she hadn't mastered the sign rules. I saw on her first Test that her processes were all good, she just missed every negative sign, sometimes using different not correct sign rules on the same problem.

She was a very smart girl, whose confidence was lacking because of a gap in her knowledge. You have seen this same thing many times, right? Low confidence caused from a low level of success in prior classes.

We all know that once they begin to apply the rules correctly, their grade always goes up as well as their confidence. It is probably a good idea to remove all gaps in knowledge, every time you can. Once the obstacles are gone, there is nothing holding them back.

Therefore, what movie clip are you thinking of right now? Hmm, let us see, we need a character that breaks through whatever is holding them back, be it math rules, or anything else in their life that has become an obstacle and they're off and running. You thought of the same one I did, didn't you? Run Forrest Run....

Affirmation: I am a genius and I apply my wisdom.

12

5TH TIMES A CHARM

All of our students have gaps in their knowledge. Maybe they do not have the multiplication tables down pat, their spelling needs help, they are not reading on grade level, or any other subject from prior years is lacking.

They tell me all the time in math that their past teacher never taught them the topic I am expecting them to know. Sometimes it is just an excuse, but it is still possible that some will have a gap in knowledge.

The official name for this gap is *LACK OF REFERENTIAL INDEX*. Our brains use a filing system. After going to a few football games no one will ask questions like, "What's a first down?" or "Why do they call it yards rushing?" or "How many points is a touchdown?"

After watching a handful of games either in person or on television, a *REFERENTIAL INDEX* is formed. I am sure the average person has many thousands of *REFERENTIAL INDEXES* they have created over their span of their life.

When we like things a lot or they have a greater level of importance, we create a better and more complex *REFERENTIAL INDEX*. For example, I have a giant *REFERENTIAL INDEX* for stories from the Bible and an extremely small one for foreign languages. I was more interested in the Bible than I was in foreign languages.

My *REFERENTIAL INDEX* in mathematics is also huge. I love it, so it is easier for me to think that all my students could love it as much as I do. They do not.

So it is only natural their *REFERENTIAL INDEX* for

math is smaller than mine. It could even be very tiny.

When some teen tells me that they have never done very good in prior math classes and it is their least favorite subject, what I hear them say is their *REFERENTIAL INDEX* needs building up. My question to test their *REFERENTIAL INDEX* is, "Have you always made an A in other math classes?" The look on their face is sometimes priceless as is their answer, as they will describe just how strong their *REFERENTIAL INDEX* is, or is not.

Okay! So all I need is some way to get them to create a massive *REFERENTIAL INDEX* for math and make them like it at the same time. Is that all?

All teachers face this issue. We can say, oh well, beats me, and leave them behind, or not. What to do? I have tried any number of ways to improve the strength of their *REFERENTIAL INDEX.* Some ideas have worked and others have not. Hang with me and I will share my favorite.

In all of my college math classes, anytime a problem seemed hard or I didn't totally understand the problem, I would just keep doing the same problem until all the fog cleared and I understood it completely. The 5th time seemed to be the charm.

Therefore, to help my students remove all fog and gaps in knowledge I have them do all reviews 5 times for a bonus of 10 points. Not all of them will do the review 5 times, although the A students almost always do.

On Test retakes, the requirement to retake a Test is to do corrections 5 times. If the retest is done within one week from when the test is returned, the new grade is multiplied by .9, and by .7 if taken after one week. The new grade stands even if it is lower.

Doing a problem 5 times might be enough, but when it's not, just continuing to practice it until the fog clears is the suggested course to pump up a *REFERENTIAL INDEX.* It is amazing how the repetition helps solidify all prior mathematical concepts.

The final exam review is always a good barometer of the building up of their *REFERENTIAL INDEX*. When the 77 problem review for the final, which is made up of problems from the 450 pages that were covered, is actually done 5 times, 2 things have always happened. The review that they turn in is very thick and there is a high grade on the final exam.

Hmm... I wonder how many other ways we could make our students *REFERENTIAL INDEX* grow?

Affirmation: I am a genius and I apply my wisdom.

13

TO THE NINES - PART 1

We left Austin on November 14, 2005 to take our son Neal to the Mayo Clinic in Rochester, Minnesota, for some tests. He was not in very good shape. They did everything that they could for Neal. Unfortunately, there was not much that could be done at that point. Neal was a real fighter for about another 6 months before God, in his wisdom, saved him from any more suffering and took him home on July 7, 2006.

The doctors at Mayo are extremely impressive. They group think all major decisions. When the specialists make rounds at the hospital they would not come by themselves but in a group. It was fairly common for 5 or 6 doctors to show up, one being an intern, one a staff doctor, and the rest specialists in their field of medicine. They do this so that they all have their own *frame of reference,* as opposed to just reading a patients file. They want to see the patient themselves. I believe that this is the reason they are the gold standard in medicine. They are all brilliant. They make many major decisions as a group.

We in education could probably learn something from this approach. What I got out of it, however, was something entirely different from group decision making. I was stressed out, not sleeping much, shaving only every other day and generally looking very haggardly. I just wanted to change my mental outlook and feel better, that was all. Before the experiment I was planning was over, to my surprise, I got far more than I expected.

My good friend and mentor Ross Meredith died the week after Christmas, 2005. He was 82. Ross was an awesome storyteller. He made me laugh even though I might have had heard the story he was telling many times. His wife Rosemary, labeled Gabby by one of her granddaughters, asked me to assist with Ross' memorial service. She did not know it, of course, but she actually sped up the experiment I had been planning. So did her son in law when he put his hand in my pocket and left some cash. Thank you so much, he said.

I have no idea just how many ways we could react when we get stressed to the max? At times, we handle it okay and other times we do not. Unfortunately, many issues wind up being out of our control. Medical issues are just one of many. Students that refuse our help and insist on not doing their work is another. Decisions the administration above us makes that might affect us in some way might be another source of stress. Trouble at home, at times, stresses us.

Our jobs are too often stressful. Our lives away from work can be too. Therefore, how we choose to deal with all of our stresses is, in the final analysis, up to us. What techniques do you commonly use when the stresses pile up? Make a list. One of my old ones from my past is go to the movies as an escape. Even though I knew the stress would still be there when I left the theatre, it was always worth the 2-hour escape. The key is to do something. Maybe it will help and maybe it won't, so do it anyway and see what happens.

Now, there was no turning back. It was time to execute my plan. I got busy on my little project to change my mental outlook and feel better. It changed more than just my mental outlook, too, all thanks to the doctors at Mayo, who were helping me, without realizing that they were even helping me. Hmm? I found a great stress reducer. Thanks Mayo!

Looking back, I was just trying to find a way to cope. I was never mad at God about Neal being so sick, just weary. I needed a change, so here's what I did.

Affirmation: I am a genius and I apply my wisdom.

14

TO THE NINES - PART 2

During the 20 years of Neal's life, we spent days, weeks and sometimes months at a time in the hospital. Most all the doctors wore the traditional white coat. We did not see a single white coat at the Mayo clinic. They were all dressed to the nines. They all wore what appeared to be high-end dress clothes, the expensive stuff. They appeared to be dressed up for a night on the town, or on their way to some extra special occasion.

The first day of school in January I showed up dressed to the nines. I felt different all right. I was asked no less than 20 times that day if I had a job interview. Every female teacher or secretary I encountered that day commented on how nice I looked. Thank you, I said politely. My ego loved the attention I have to admit.

My students wanted to know why I was dressed up. I would say that I just decided to dress up, as my students are on a need to know basis with me. They didn't need to know any more than that.

The first week of the semester, I noticed that the students were more serious about their work. More of them were actually doing their homework. This was shocking. I'm wearing a suit, so you do more homework? I was baffled, as I was just trying to change my mental outlook and feel better.

My students were paying attention. They were curious as to my purpose. Since I had refused to say the real reason I started dressing up, they kept after me to tell them *my little secret*. I did not want to reveal that I was just trying to change my mental outlook so I would feel better.

At the beginning of class one day a nice young man went to the board, picked up the marker, made a multiple choice question, and had the whole class vote on what they thought was the real reason I was dressing up. It looked something like this:

Why did Mr. Massie start dressing up?
A. He wants us to be more serious about our work.
B. He wants more respect.
C. His wife is making him dress up.
D. He won the lottery.
E. He is working on a research project.
F. He is going to many job interviews.

I can't remember which one had the most votes. It was probably A. I told them that the real reason was not on their list. I just wanted to feel better. I wanted to change my mental outlook. I never told them the real reason. They didn't need to know.

They had also made a very powerful point. They notice everything! They knew unconsciously that I had been struggling and was stressed. They had given me a pass on that one due to the circumstances involved with Neal being so sick. They also proved that it is a fact that teenagers assign a motive to everything we do. They are wrong most all the time, but they assign a motive just the same.

If I come to class dressed "slouchy", they are not going to take me as seriously. If I do not care how I look, how much do I really care about my job as their teacher or myself as a person? They know what slouchy means, even though they prefer to dress that way, they really expect more out of authority figures. They should, too, shouldn't they?

They have an internal scale of 1 to 10 for every teacher.

They know who is mean, and who is not, according to them. They know who is married and who is just living with someone. Each student has their own way of deciding who they respect, and just how much they respect each teacher.

Right now, you are wondering if it worked, right? Did my mental outlook change? Did I feel any better? Was my stressed relieved to any degree? Was the whole idea just a crazy attempt to distract my stress, or what? What happened? The transformation was remarkable.

Affirmation: I am a genius and I apply my wisdom.

15

TO THE NINES – PART 3

The results of my little experiment include the following positive changes in my life, in no particular order:

1. I feel much better.
2. My mental outlook changed. I am more serious about my job.
3. My dressing up reminds me that I have a very important job.
4. My students are more serious about their work.
5. I have more respect than before.
6. Some parents are intimidated by the way I am dressed.
7. People hold doors for me everywhere I go, both in school and out.
8. Women compliment my pink tie. Why don't more men wear pink? This one makes me smile.
9. All the women in our building, at one time or another, have commented on my dressing up. I was not counting on getting so much female attention, but am learning to live with it. Lol.
10. Several men in our building have asked me where to buy a good suit.
11. I smile more.
12. I notice what other people are wearing more than before.
13. I get asked if I even own a pair of blue jeans.
14. During staff development days this year, several teachers said they hardly recognized me without the

suit.

15. Every formal evaluation always has a comment about me being professionally dressed.
16. My principal asked me where he can get a "peach" shirt like mine.
17. When I eat out and am dressed up, I get fantastic service. They think I am important. I am.
18. Some people think that I am rich, because I wear expensive looking clothes. Are you a banker, a judge, or a lawyer? LOL

The change of dress achieved its intended outcome. I felt better. I had a higher level of self-respect. Although it took a while, I got used to being dressed up. Today suits made from merino wool are lightweight and are as comfortable as a jogging suit. I am glad I began dressing up.

Take every opportunity to touch the lives of all your students. Dressing up will actually be fun. In addition, when you come to the end of your last year in the classroom, you will most likely stand in the doorway of your room and pause to reflect on all the time spent there. I have done what the character from *Mr. Holland's Opus*, Mr. Holland, did each time I left one school to move to another. Remember, he stood in the doorway and stared into his band hall remembering students and events that happened there. Whoever wrote the script for *Mr. Holland's Opus* found out a lot of things that teachers experience. Makes we wonder who his teacher consultants were?

Although it might be nicer to know the real impact we have had on so many lives, know that it is very wide and deep. At least in *Mr. Holland's Opus* he got to see it. We may or may not be so lucky.

Affirmation: I am a genius and I apply my wisdom.

16

TO THE NINES – PART 4
BUILDING A WARDROBE

Here are a few suggestions as you build your dress wardrobe. Ladies, ya'll are much better at this than us guys, so keep doing what you're doing. So for the men......

1. You can afford to dress up every day. You might even spend less on clothes than you normally do.
2. Set some goals for your dress wardrobe. Mine were to buy 3 suits at the beginning and then one every summer and eventually get to where I had 10. I got there in year 8.
3. Some solid colors will allow for a lot of flexibility. You might consider solid black, navy and charcoal gray suits. The slacks can be worn with most any sports coat and can be mixed and matched with each other. Add a pair of tan dress slacks.
4. I started slow with dress shirts and discovered I really liked the Gold Label Roundtree and Yorke dress shirts from Dillard's. The half price dress shirt sale is around the first of the year. Use some Christmas money and get 4 for $100 at the Dillard's sale every year. It won't take very many years to have more than 20. I rotate them in my closet and wind up wearing each one about once a month. The quality of these shirts is great and they last a long time.
5. Silk ties can be bought for less than $10, or sometimes even $5. I found some on sale at the London airport one time and got 10 for $30. Ebay is another good resource

for ties. The proverbial wisdom in the book Dress for Success, which I highly recommend, is that we should let our wives pick out our ties, but not our suits. Whatever! Actually this has worked really well for me as my wife is an artist and picks out great ties, which I would never have even considered. Get a few with bright colors. I have one lime green one that my students say is loud. I tell them I keep it plugged in so it will stay charged up.

6. My students think I have 50 suits and blazers. LOL! This is because a different shirt and tie combination makes it look that way.

7. Jos A Banks online is where I buy suits, sport coats and blazers. I only do so when the clearance suit prices get to about $100. You will not find these prices in any store. Just be patient and look at the clearance page when the summer comes. They will all be marked down that low, eventually. When you take one out of the box the tag will say $495, $795, $995, or $1,295, when you only paid $100, this will make you smile.

So let's see, one suit, 4 dress shirts and 5 ties per year should run about $240. You can dress up every day for $20 per month, or 66 cents a day. You will feel better. You will get more respect! People will hold doors open for you, both in and out of school. Women will say you look nice. You will! I think you'll love dressing up.

You might want to begin dressing up one day a week, maybe Monday, or not. What might happen if you dressed up every Monday? Would it have any effect on your week, or not? Hmm.....

If you smile constantly for however many minutes it takes, you will feel better on the inside. If you change the way you are dressed because you want to feel better, you will eventually feel better on the inside.

This universal truth goes both ways, if you change the outside the inside follows suit and if you change the inside the outside follows suit, too.

Change either the inside or the outside, your choice, it definitely worked for me.

Affirmation: I am a genius and I apply my wisdom.

17

CUSSED OUT ON THE PHONE

One day during Algebra 1 there was a student whose behavior was out of control. I had already tried several of my usual and customary techniques to get him to settle down and nothing had worked.

It was time for the main course, big bazooka, whole enchilada, my biggest weapon and card to play. I asked him to go pick up the phone on the wall and call his mother. He told me he would be glad to call her, as she would cuss me out big time. He picked up the phone, called his mother and handed me the phone.

I told her who I was, that her son was misbehaving in class and that I needed her help. She asked to talk to him. I handed him the phone.

She began yelling at him, you could hear it all over the room. She used almost every curse word I have ever heard. She was very mad. He had the phone about 6 inches from his ear and kept saying, "Yes Mam." My room was very quiet. Everyone heard what this mom was saying. She finally asked to talk to me again.

She was extremely sweet on the phone as her tone made a 180 degree shift. She said to please call her if I had any more trouble with him. I said that I would and said goodbye.

The young man asked if he could talk to me out in the hall. OK. He wanted me to promise that I would never call his mother again. I told him that if his behavior was perfect that I would have no reason to call her and that I would not, as long as he kept his behavior in check and did his homework. He held out his hand to shake mine. We had a deal.

His behavior was perfect for the rest of the year. So was everyone else's, as no one was willing to run the risk that I would call their mother during class.

How many other ways can we get the parents to help us correct unruly behavior? I am not sure, but calling a parent during class has always worked for me, after all other attempts have failed.

I do not do this one very often. I use it only when necessary. I have never had a parent refuse to help me get behavior in check. They have seen their kids pull the same kind of stuff at home. They do not want to put up with it either. They most always have apologized to me, said they are so sorry that I have been treated that way and asked me to call them whenever I need to.

Get the parents on your side. If you expect them to help you, there is an excellent chance that they will. Most parents tell their teens that they had better not get any calls from school. When they hear me asking for their help, they suspect that I have already tried everything else and are very glad to oblige.

I put on an act the following day and pretended that nothing happened. I caught the student looking at me wondering if I was going to hold it against him for the rest of his life. When I do not hold it against them, they go with whatever I ask them to do from then on, which is what I wanted in the first place.

Do whatever it takes to control your classroom and keep all distractions to an absolute minimum.

Affirmation: I am a genius and I apply my wisdom.

18

MISS PRICE TATTLES ON ME

One year I had a student named Miss Price. She was feisty. Things went smoothly the first 6 weeks of school. Then they changed our wing to split lunch. The class would go for about an hour, break for lunch for 30 minutes, and return for the 2nd part of class for an additional 30 minutes.

Miss Price began to be late every day from split lunch. She would come in late with food from a local fast food place and demand to eat it during the 2nd part of class. I would say no dice. She would argue. I would say you are already late so sit outside in the hall and eat it.

I eventually wrote a referral when she got the 8th tardy. A couple of days later somebody from the office came to my room saying I needed to come down to our main office and speak with Miss Price's mother. When I arrived she was in a conference room with her daughter and 2 of our counselors.

After introductions were made the mom attacked. "Is it true that you told my daughter that she could not go to the restroom for the rest of the school year?" She was fired up. Everyone looked at me for my response.

I said," I do not actually recall what I told her. Is that what she is saying I said?" Yes, she said. "Then, yes, I told her she could not go to the restroom for the rest of the school year."

The mother looked shocked, as she must have been expecting me to deny it and launch the argument to another level.

She asked me why I would have ever told her daughter something like that. I explained all the tardies from lunch, all the food she was wanting to bring into my room, how only seniors are allowed to go off campus and she was a junior and that I had a sign on my bulletin board for classroom procedures that said if there is any monkey business in the hall when you are out of the room, that all privileges would be revoked until the end of the year, including going to the restroom.

The mom turned and started ripping into her daughter. Why was she leaving campus? Miss Price lied and said another student was bringing food to her. "This man has a sign on his wall. You are disrupting his class."

The mom explained to me how sorry she was for her daughter being out of control, that she was glad to get the real story and that I should call her if there was any more trouble. They politely excused themselves and left the room.

When I started to leave the counselors asked me if I could stay for a minute. They wanted to know how I had diffused the situation so quickly. They acted as if they had never seen anything like it. Really?

I told them that I do not let parents push me around. I refuse to argue with students or parents. All my rules are very clear and posted for all to see. If you break them then get ready for the stated consequence. I was not about to let them push me around over going off campus for lunch, running out of time, and then demanding to eat lunch after lunch was over.

I was very nice to the mother, just forceful with my comments. I was also in a suit and tie and could tell that it was intimidating to her.

Miss Price was perfect for the rest of the year.

Two years passed, and during the first week of January, we were in school, the colleges had not yet started and one afternoon Miss Price walked into my room. She had come to visit. She said that because I made her show all the steps of the long Pre-Calculus problems, that she had made an A in College Algebra. She was one of the few students in her class that could show all the work when the problems stretched to a page or longer. She had grown up a lot and just wanted to come see me.

It was great to see her. I did have to defriend her from Facebook because she was posting 5 times a day, but that is another matter for another day. I have a Facebook policy. I only agree to add a friend after they are out of high school. If they post too much I defriend them.

It has always been the case that when we, as teachers, have our students follow our class rules and they know we mean business, that they will come around and appreciate the structure. It always gives us more respect, even if they fuss about it. Do not be surprised when they come back to see you either. We all know that is only because they have a higher level of respect for you.

Weekend Update: We were at a birthday party at Fuddrucker's last March. Wouldn't you know that Miss Price just happened to be there, too. We saw each other and caught up a bit. She has been out of college for 2 years and is back at her high school as a faculty member. I am proud of her. She is out there making a difference in the world.

Affirmation: I am a genius and I apply my wisdom.

19

PAUL'S MOM LOWERS THE BOOM

I had Paul is class one year. He was very extroverted. He seemed to be constantly in trouble, made too much noise, talked way too much, didn't stay on top of his work, etc.

I had already moved his seating assignment a time or two. Things got to the point where I needed to call his mother. I called her during my conference period. She asked if she could come to the next class meeting, which was fine with me. I told her the next class meeting was Test day. She said that was okay with her, that she looked forward to meeting me.

When she came into class Paul ducked down real low. He felt the pressure and was generally looking guilty. His mother and I sat down up front at the conference table. She started to talk in a whisper that could be heard all over the room.

She said she was on the war path about his behavior. He knew better and she was not going to put up with his unruly behavior any more. She said that as a single parent she had trouble with both Paul and his younger sister. She got pretty fired up as she talked. She was determined that her kids would become positive members of society and make something of their lives. She was not going to accept anything less.

She launched into a diatribe on the use of their cell phones. She said that every night at 8 pm the cell phones better be on the kitchen table. Each day she goes through all of their text messages. If anything has been erased she asks what it is that they didn't want their mom to see. Her discourse was so funny it was all I could do to control myself and not laugh.

Then she described how she straightened her daughter out the year before. She said her daughter was out of control. When she came to school to pick her up one day, she got out of the car, met her daughter, headed into the building and didn't stop until she found a policeman. We had 3 full time policemen on our campus at all times. She asked the policeman to take his hand cuffs out, put them on her daughter and escort them to the campus principal's office.

When they got there she demanded that her daughter be assigned to our Alternative School for 30 days, because her behavior was out of control. The principal explained that usually a student's school behavior was the determining factor in an assignment to the Alternative School. She said she wanted her daughter sent there for 30 days and wasn't going take no for an answer.

A 30-day assignment was given to the alternative school. The mom thought it was great that her daughter had to wear black pants and a white t-shirt for 30 days. She then took what she called all her daughter's "shorty shorts, short skirts, and tight fitting jeans" and donated them to Goodwill. If her daughter wanted to "strut her stuff", she said, she would have to get a job and buy the clothes herself. Mom was done playing games. The result was that her daughter's behavior changed and according to mom, she was like a different person.

She said that now it was Paul's turn and she was determined to get him in line, too. She did.

I had no more trouble with Paul. He would occasionally get a little bit rowdy, due to his extroverted nature and all I had to do was ask him if we needed to get his mom on the phone and he would get quiet.

Her description of how she had gotten control of her kids was the funniest thing I have ever heard a parent describe. She is a fantastic speaker, has a master's degree and I'm thinking a new career in speaking to parents about getting their teenagers in line. I asked her if she would be willing to come speak to parents if we set something up and she agreed. I passed her contact information on to our administration.

Unfortunately, it is the case that some of our students are running their households. I have had many parents tell me that they are sick of their kids and do not know what to do with them. Just waiting on them to get old enough to leave home is not correcting any of their unruly behavior. It is admittedly hard to practice tough love on your own children. Sometimes tough love is the only answer.

Therefore, maybe we should all do a better job working with the parents of our students. When we get on the same page as mom and dad, all wanting what's in the best long term interest of any teenager, the expectations get set. There is not any guarantee that unruly behavior will be corrected, but there is a higher probability that it will, than if we do nothing.

So when students become difficult to deal with, what will you do to attempt to correct unruly behavior? How many ways can you send a message to their parents that you care about them? How many different ways could a teacher work with parents to assist a student to grow out of unruly behavior or non-productive decisions?

My suggestion is to call the parents and ask for their help. Describe the behavior you are seeking to correct. Ask them what ideas they have. When they ask me, I always say something like, "What is so important to them, if you took it away for a week, it would get their attention?" I usually hear something like, "Oh that's good, I can ground their cell phone for a week or more!" or, "Is it possible to have texting blocked from every number except mine?"

The father of another one of my students asked to see his daughter's keys one day when she got home from school. He was standing on the driveway talking to some man. The next thing the girl knew the man had bought her truck and was driving it off their property. Her dad said, if you cannot behave, then you don't need any wheels. Go figure. He did me a big favor. I had no more trouble with her after he sold her truck. All the back talking stopped and she began making A's on everything. Build bridges with all the parents you can. Just saying.

Affirmation: I am a genius and I apply my wisdom.

20

BITING A GIRLS HEAD OFF

One day in Pre-Cal I bit a girls head off, figuratively speaking. It was one of those stressed out days when my nerves were shot. I was terse, agitated, and hyped up all day. When she said something, I attacked. What she said was not even really that out of line. After I chewed on her awhile, she responded with, "That was uncalled for!"

I went on with class pretending that nothing had happened. Everyone knew she was right. Me pretending that I had not been out of line didn't change the facts.

I had 2 choices. I could pretend that nothing had happened, or I could apologize. Hmm. What to do?

I apologized to both the girl and the class. When I did, I got many strange looks. I asked if anybody wanted to say anything. The girl said I was forgiven! Another student asked why teachers would almost never apologize when they were wrong. Are we too proud? Maybe we don't ever want to show any chinks in our armor. We had an interesting short discussion after my apology.

We are not perfect. When we make errors, making amends is always a good idea. We lose respect for sure, when we are arrogant to the point we will not admit fault. We will lose less respect if we apologize when we should.

As Steven Covey says in all his books, *"IF YOU KEEP ON DOING WHAT YOU'VE ALWAYS DONE, YOU'LL KEEP GETTING WHAT YOU'VE ALWAYS GOTTEN."*

So, when something doesn't go the way it should, we must be willing to change; change a lesson, change a behavior, change an assignment, change an outlook, change a relationship, change an attitude, change a viewpoint and change anything that needs changing. Our students already know and so do we, so what is the big deal.

I wonder how many ways we could be losing respect? How many of those could we change? And of course, is there anything hanging around out there that we didn't apologize for, yet?

Affirmation: I am a genius and I apply my wisdom.

21

AM I CONVINCED, YET?

Everyone has a convincer strategy. It is an unconscious filter. You started yours a long time ago. You unconsciously use it as a gage, so to speak, in order to be totally convinced. Although the context may switch, most likely, your convincer strategy will probably never change, unless you decided to change it, of course.

Your convincer strategy could include a number of times, or a period of time, or maybe both. You made it up, so it works perfectly, however you did it.

For the number of times, how many times would you have to see me do something in an excellent way, before you were totally convinced I was good at it? Would once be enough? Is your convincer strategy instantaneous? Or would you have to see me do it in an excellent way, 2,3,4,5,6,7,8,9,...... or however many times in a row, before you were totally convinced that I was good at it?

Say the number out loud or write it in the margin. How many? Would that really do it for you? Or, would you need to wait for some period of time before you were convinced?

For example, I have a friend who has heard me speak before a group of 200 over 100 times. Her convincer strategy number is 6. Six times, should have been enough for her to be convinced, right? Nope, not exactly, because she also has a time period built into her convincer strategy. It is 6 months. 6 times and 6 months. If I had bombed a speech during the 6 months, she would have never been convinced.

When 6 months had passed, she was convinced that I was

okay, both as a speaker and as a friend. I could tell something was different, too. Actually, you always know when someone thinks you are all right, as you know it unconsciously. On many levels, the reservation is gone, along with most skepticism. You made it passed the door, so to speak. They have let you come inside a bit, so to speak. They are convinced that you can be trusted and are excellent at whatever they have seen you do.

If you are a teacher like me, you know consciously when any student has let you inside. How long did it take them to trust you? They might only have a number in their convincer strategy. They might just have a period of time. They can have both. It is whatever it is, isn't it?

So think about your students. I mean the ones that you have right now. Have they all let you in? Maybe even more important, is their convincer strategy keeping them from believing that they are excellent mathematicians?

If their convincer strategy is a number like 11, then they would have to be excellent 11 times in a row, before they became convinced that they were a genius in math.

If you guessed that the number 11 was from one of my students, then you are way ahead of me. This little girl had low confidence in Algebra 2. She, according to her, had never been any good at math. One day when we were practicing problems, doing my practicing routine, I asked her how many problems in a row she would have to get right, before she was totally convinced that she was a genius at math. She said 11.

I was shocked. That is a big number. So, I started the countdown. As they were bringing their papers, I would say when she got one right, that's 1, only 10 more and you are a genius. I kept the countdown going all the way to 11. She was extremely perplexed when she got through. She was not supposed to be a genius in math, according to her. Now the proof was there beside her name in my grade book. Eleven in a row were correct.

"What are you doing to me?" she said. "Nothing", I said, "but, you just proved what I already knew, which is the indisputable fact that you are a genius in the field of math." When she did not argue the point, it was feedback that her convincer strategy was satisfied.

She made A's the rest of the school year, because she was convinced she was a math genius.

All teachers of all subjects know students whose confidence is low. More often than not, I may have lost the battle to get them to convince themselves that they are excellent. I do not know if it is because they just go through the motions in what they would call their worst subject, or not?

They fulfill their own convincer strategy, whatever it is. If they are convinced that they will pass or fail, whichever one it is, they are right.

Convincer strategies are very interesting to me. I believe that art and foreign language are my weakest subjects. I believe that I could change this belief. I need to get out of my own way, so would you be so kind as to hand me that paint brush, por favor?

Affirmation: I am a genius and I apply my wisdom.

22

CHUNK AND SEQUENCE

NLP Trainer Training was a steep learning curve for me. Training the unconscious mind involves so many things that you need to do simultaneously. I felt like I was being overwhelmed. I was right. It is very overwhelming.

It also was embarrassing. What made it so embarrassing was the truth that I had been bombing a lot over the years, when speaking to all sizes of groups at both church and school. I tried to console myself with the rationalization that I did not really know what I was supposed to be doing, so I needed to give myself a pass.

The truth was I had missed hundreds of opportunities. I would never get those back. It was a sobering realization. I had no excuses left, since I knew what I needed to do. This was very humbling.

I must change, whether I wanted to, or not. If it was comfortable, or not. If I liked it, or not. I was determined to re-invent myself. The good news was that *everything* needed to change, so there were plenty of places to start.

I began by shifting my focus. It zeroed in on chunking and sequencing. It is the best place to begin, I thought.

The chunk size is the easiest to fix. One little chunk at a time. One little bite. I can still hear Dr. Dan's voice as he would say, "The material must be chunked at a gradient where it is impossible to not succeed." I began learning how to turn whatever I was teaching into bite size pieces.

The reason that chunk size is the best place to start is because it is the most common mistake that all teachers and speakers make. We have this tendency to give them the whole pan of enchiladas at once, which usually puts them on overwhelm, they tune us out, which leads to even more material and then to even more material. More all at once is not always better.

So, I gave my students one little chunk. Only when they had mastered that chunk did they get the next most logical chunk in the sequence, where it is easiest for their unconscious minds to get it quickly.

The process I used in Algebra I began calling "lecture short and work long". I would show them two examples and then have them do as many similar problems as it took for the whole room to get it. Then two examples on the next chunk, and so on.

It was a big surprise to me that we could actually move through the material faster, partly because I very rarely had to re-explain something they could not remember how to do. The feedback was that they really did have all the prior chunks mastered. So, we were going through the material faster. This was interesting.

They were also all succeeding. It was impossible to do otherwise. This was a whole new world that I had not yet experienced before. I liked it a lot. The students had not seen anything like it either. They liked it, too.

Each day when I go to work, as the day is unfolding, my planning is focused on the chunks I will be teaching that day. When everyone in the room has caught up and has it, we move ahead. Today, August 25, 2011, we cycled through 3 chunks in Pre-Calculus. They did a very good job. Most of them had already unconsciously gone on to the next piece even before I got ready to go there, which was amazing.

I am sure that you can get more leverage with chunk and sequence than any other single change you could possibly make with whatever subject you teach. Your class will never go on overwhelm again, as soon as the material is chunked at a gradient where it is impossible to not succeed.

You can cover all the material your state requires of you by adapting your planning to chunk and sequence. You will actually cover it faster. It will be more fun for both you and your students. Get the chunk size down to just one bite. When they have that bite, do the next chunk on your list. Allow enough time to gauge when they have it, then move on. Cover as many chunks as you can each day. Lecture short and make them practice.

Keep on going.

Pay a lot of attention to the sequence, or order of topics. What's the next most logical piece of material? What should follow that piece? You already know your material, so line it up in the best brain friendly order, according to you.

I am forced to change my semester outlines often. Some topics take less time than I thought and some take more time. Adjusting on the fly will actually be easy.

I cover every topic that is required by the Texas Essential Knowledge and Skills, or TEKS. I cover some over 2 or 3 days and sometimes 3 in one day. When the students have it, it's time to move on. When they don't have it, yet, it's time to practice a little more.

The best thing you can do is to never move on to the next topic, until they have mastered the current one. That's our biggest mistake, running ahead and leaving them behind.

Chunk it at a gradient where it is impossible to not succeed. You can do it. Fun awaits.

Affirmation: I am a genius and I apply my wisdom.

23

THE MISSING LINKS

What were we missing? It seems for years when working with our students to prepare them to take the state assessment Test, that each year we would work harder than ever before and when the scores came back we would have only moved a percentage point or two. At times, the central office curriculum department would throw a party to reward us for all of our hard work and for our fantastic success. On the inside I would be wondering what we were missing?

A 2-percentage point change could just be the difference in this group of juniors over last year's group. We had no control set up, like they do in a real experiment. From a statistical standpoint, the control on something like our state assessments would be to do nothing, the question being, if we did nothing and the scores went up 2 points, we would conclude that the change was just the difference in this year's group of juniors.

It is much easier to set a control when doing a drug study to test migraine medicine. The control group will get the sugar pill. How would we set up a control anyway for something like the State Assessment Test? I was wondering just what I might do to make the scores rise higher?

What I did worked, as the scores of my students shot up 17 points the following year. Actually, I can't take much credit, as I just did what Dr. Dan taught me to do. Left to my own I would have never known to make the changes that were necessary to make the scores shoot up so much.

Instinctively every math teacher I have ever known, knows that when they are grading a student's paper that some of the students will miss a problem that we know they know how to do. We have regular discussions about the answers that our students got on last year's State Assessment Test. We look at them and always seem to find a kid we know understands how to do a specific problem misses it. Why do they do that?

Our solution for years has been to work the curriculum harder the next year. The next year almost nothing changes. So, we work the curriculum even harder and hardly anything changes again.

Surely hiring a curriculum coach would be of help? We hired some and still not much changed. Then we hired some instructional coaches to work specifically with our teachers and not much changed. Then the school improvement group came in and figured out what the department chair already knew, which was that some of our teachers were not cutting it. Some teaching positions changed around and still not much changed.

When my scores jumped 17 percentage points I was shocked and elated. No one asked me why the big jump. The next year we beat the school average again by double digits, and no one asked why. The only reason I found the answer to the question, "What are we missing?" was because I went and did what Dr. Dan taught me to do.

The truth is that after you have been trained in the art and science of Neuro Linguistic Programming your eyes will be opened. Once they are opened you will not be able to not see what is really going on. What was the real reason that the scores were not going up by double digits across the board?

Actually, if you think about it, the system being used has already proven that we do not have a curriculum problem. We have been hammering the curriculum so hard the last 10 years, if the problem was really about curriculum, we would have already taken a big step forward. There are not double digits gains to be had just by working the curriculum harder. The truth is we were working the curriculum as hard as possible already. The good thing is that all the hard work has kept us where we are. So keep working the curriculum just as hard as ever? That is right. Then if we want a double digit jump in scores, add in the pieces we were missing.

Okay, so if the problem is not content based, you are thinking, what is it? It is process. It is our process. And even more importantly it is the student's process. I went to the only place one could go to find out the answer to what were we missing, I went and asked my students. Duh.

It was embarrassing. The question we have not been asking is all about what taking the State Assessment Test looks like through the student's eyes? So I asked them questions like: What is it like to take the State Assessment Test? What are you thinking as you take it? What would help you do even a better job? Are you expecting to make a high score?

I asked them any and every question I could think to ask, and just listened. Their answers were weighted heavily towards process. There were some statements about the kinds of problems they didn't like, but most statements were about the process of the whole thing. Three giant problems were uncovered as I listened to their description of what it was like to take a Math State Assessment Test.

The three main problems the students talked about were, in no particular order; lack of confidence, being overwhelmed by the material and fatigue from sitting so long. We were preparing them from a content basis as best as we possibly could. We were not cutting it in the areas of building confidence, stopping fatigue and eliminating being overwhelmed by the material.

All righty then, as soon as we made their confidence soar, stopped them from getting overwhelmed by the material and kept fatigue from happening we would be off and running to new heights. Is that all? How could we accomplish it? Doing nothing was not an option. So here we go.

Affirmation: I am a genius and I apply my wisdom.

24

HOW TO MAKE CONFIDENCE SOAR

As described in the last chapter one major problem the students have when taking the State Assessment Test has to do with their level of confidence. Low confidence leads to low scores. Duh. Just how to make confidence go up became the issue.

The student's confidence issue was simply that too many had never had much success taking a State Assessment Test. Some of them had a level of defeatism before the test was given. If they were expecting to not do very well on the test they wound up getting what they expected. What had to happen for them to become confident?

I had my work cut out for me. I came up with a plan, put it in motion, and the first year the test scores jumped 17 percentage points. The next year it needed some tweaking, so adjustments were made. After 3 or 4 years things settled down and I learned that the whole process could be learned fairly quickly, like 3 to 4 weeks. Cool.

You could actually wait to start training them to pass the State Assessment Test until the 1st of April, although I only did so once. Our normal routine was to begin working on the State Assessment Test in August. I wanted to test how much of a factor time was. Did I really need to spend so much time in the fall semester working on a Test that would be given in May? So one year I waited until April 1 to begin working on the State Assessment Test. That year 68 of 71 of my Geometry students passed. This was more confirmation to me that they had enough content down to ace the State

Assessment Test and that I could take care of conquering any lack of confidence in a month. I only waited to start training them one year, as it is important to make them as confident as possible as soon as possible.

What needed to happen for them to become confident? The students are all over the map on this one. There are many different levels of confidence or the lack thereof in any one class at the same time. I selected "pattern interrupt" as the method to make their confidence soar to new heights.

If a student was already confident then that was great, as I would not have to worry as much about the ones that already were confident. However, to convince someone who is not confident to become confident is a very different proposition. The not yet confident ones all have some pattern they run that is a first cousin to defeatism. They know they will not excel on a test because they never have, so they go in expecting to not pass and when they do not pass they are not surprised.

If you do not break the old pattern of non-confidence then they will do what they have been doing and their grade could remain low. It is imperative that you focus on making "pattern interrupt" work. You must take the responsibility to interrupt the old defeatism pattern. It is actually pretty easy. I think you will like it.

"Pattern Interrupt" is an NLP term. The NLP guys say that it takes between 7 and 21 times of having success to break an old pattern. So, I aimed high figuring that sometime in the first 50 times or so, most of them would break their old pattern. Yes, I know what you are thinking, and you are right, the student has to break his own old defeatism pattern. Your job will be to watch them like a hawk, which is actually amusing at times, as this messes with them.

They begin having success and will first think it is just an accident, since it isn't supposed to be happening. Then they will move to the puzzled stage as you can see the puzzling look on their faces. Somewhere in there they will look almost shell shocked as they are being very successful, which they think is not supposed to be happening. It is all new to them. You can watch them processing the dissolution of the old pattern, until they finally give up the old one for the new successful one. More than once I have had a student ask, "What are you doing to me?" I ask, "Don't you like being successful?" They will smile and say," Well, I never have?", and I will say, "Well look at all these perfect grades, it seems like you have proven that you are successful! That's what I see!" Eventually they give it up. Going from living in defeatism for many years to all of the sudden becoming extremely successful is an enormous step, as well as perhaps, a first time experience. You want to help them experience success, which will win out over defeatism in the end.

When I see this happening, I know that the odds of the old pattern staying dead are very high. The truth is that the vast majority of all teachers have always operated from a high level of confidence. It makes it harder for us to be able to understand what it is like for the student that has lived for years in a non-confident state of defeatism. We know the ones who are not confident, but until I took NLP, just what I could do about it was outside my awareness. If you are reading this right now, you now know that there is something you must do, and that is "Pattern Interrupt"! If you do not interrupt the old pattern, the chances of them becoming confident on their own while in your class are low, as they would have to do it all by themselves. They need you to shine the light on the road to confidence.

All "Pattern Interrupt" really is, is allowing them to be successful 7 to 21 times. I do overkill and have it go 50 to 80 times just to make sure. Here is how I go about it. I freely admit that I have been pushing on your curiosity button as much as possible. How can you as a teacher make the kid that is not confident become confident because they convinced themselves that they are confident? The short story is you make them get 70 to 80 questions correct, keeping track of it as you go. Here is how I do it.

I print out 3 old State Assessment Tests for each student. I send them to our print shop. Please do not cut and paste anything. Use the paper. They need something that they can write on, just like on Test day. What you will be asking them to do needs to mirror Test day as much as possible. Just pick 3 old assessments from the state education website. Any 3 will do, although I go for the latest ones I can find.

Hand out the first Test. Have them put their name on it, then say, "Today we are just doing the problems with a Graph, a Cartesian Coordinate Plane." Start flipping through the packet and when you find one, have them answer it and put the answer on their answer key. I make answer keys about 2 inches wide by 8.5 long that just have lines on them.

We go through the entire packet just having them answering all the graphs. No discussion, no instruction, just plug through one question at a time. There are only 10 to 12 graphing questions. Have them exchange answer sheets and put the answer key on the screen so they can grade their neighbor's paper. Record the number they get correct. Make sure the number is recorded, as it will be important.

Then go over each Graphing question. I show them any and all shortcuts that I know. Use your imagination. Two of the lines are leaning left and two are leaning right, looking at the given equation you see the slope is negative, so the answer has to be leaning left. The intercept is 4, so the correct answer is the line leaning left going through 4 on the y axis. Now put the given equation into y= on your calculator, graph it and verify that you know for sure what the correct answer is. I do something like this for each question.

After you have gone over each question, take up Old Test #1. It doesn't matter how many they got right. Three to nine is normal for packet #1. Hand out packet #2, tell them to put their name on it, and do the following questions, then give them the list of all the Graphing questions in packet #2. When they get through have them bring their answer key to you, grade it real fast, record the grade and they will return to their desk. The room will get busy which is what you want. You want them to get up and move around. I'll tell you why in a few minutes. Every time I have ever done this, every student's grade has gone up on the second test. After everyone is through, go over each problem again.

For Round 3 hand out Old Test #3, and make them find the Graphing questions themselves. Grade and record the grades. One year on round 3 nobody in the entire room missed a single graphing question. Yippy Skippy! Remember that what you are really doing is working on their confidence. They will become confident with the graphing questions.

Since I am grading their answer sheet and they are standing there watching me, I always comment on how many more they got right on this round and aren't they doing great, asking them if they always made A's in all their prior math classes and telling them they are going to ace the test. I lay it on as thick as possible and watch their faces. Just how much do they believe it, at this point? Make a mental note of the look on each face, because you are watching to see that their confidence is gaining.

At this point my 90 minute class is done as we are on a block schedule. If you have shorter periods just keep going with the process tomorrow. If you teach a remediation class print off 7 old State Assessment Tests, etc.

After I am convinced that we will make a very high grade on all the Graphing questions, I am ready for category 2, which is Equations. Go through the same process with

Equations. Then proceed to Triangles, Other Geometric Figures, Tables, Word problems, etc. You are training them one category at a time. After they have been so trained, on Test day they will actually take the Test out of numerical order and place a star by each one they know is right for sure, but I'm getting ahead of myself.

Do you see "Pattern Interrupt"? I am having them do 12 questions per packet, tracking their growth and giving them all kinds of positive feedback, plus expert instruction on all kinds of ways to go right to the correct answer. I am trying to chip away at any lack of confidence.

After you have done the same process with all 8 categories their confidence will have grown tremendously. They have always wanted to pass, but never had any luck with it and just maybe they shut it down and gave up. You are giving them lots of practice with all levels of success and trust me on this, they will like this a lot, particularly those who have low confidence. They will start to wonder just how high they can go. Confidence will be high. They will attack the test.

Affirmation: I am a genius and I apply my wisdom.

25

STOPPING OVERWHELM

Overwhelm most often occurs when the students are having to answer 70 questions over 3 hours. Some students eventually get to the point where they are overwhelmed by the massive volume of the material. When they go on overwhelm even the simplest problem seems like climbing Mount Everest and they will feel the weight of the world. This leads to less confidence, according to them. The longer they work, the more overwhelmed they become and the more problems they miss.

Every year the Texas Education Agency puts out the statewide percentage correct on each assessment question. When you look at the percentage correct it begins in the 80's for the first 15 or 20 questions and then steadily drops into the 30's until the last 10 questions where it comes back a little bit. Overwhelmed by the volume of the material is real in the students model of the world.

Overwhelm disappears when the test is taken out of order by categories. This is because it is more brain friendly to only shift your context 8 times, as opposed to 70 times. So I have the students take the Test out of numerical order. They flip through the Test packet looking for graphs, as they are on a mission to achieve Commended Performance. Commended Performance means they are getting 53 out of 60 correct. The other 10 questions on the test are field test questions that TEA is trying out for the future. The field test questions increase overwhelm because they put them in the first half of the test before the students are worn out. They are not our friend. When taking the Test by categories the field test questions become irrelevant. If the Test is taken in order the field test questions will help bog your student's down.

Therefore, when a student takes the Test out of order they get, on average, 10 more questions correct. I have the data to prove it. We have consistently had 10 more questions correct than the school average. I just change all the raw scores into the number of questions correct and average. Just comparing our raw scores to the schools average raw score shows the same thing. We are getting 10 more questions correct. Since I make the kids practice flipping through packets so much before the Test while we are practicing, there is a high percentage of them that are convinced that taking the Test out of order is good for them. It is.

They also are shooting for Commended Performance so they know it will help them. The fact that they turn so many pages and still take the Test faster is further proof that they have conquered overwhelm. The truth is that after they have done the first 3 categories they have the Test passed. Having them focus on Commended Performance has them shooting way past passing. When you compare our schools average of 25% getting Commended Performance to my students who are doing 37% Commended Performance, the first thing I see is that my students never went on overwhelm.

Actually overwhelm is awful. Shifting your brain 70 times, including the 10 harder field test questions that don't count, can send our students to a place where we don't want them to go, the place where they shut it down and give in to letting the Test defeat them.

Take the Test out of order and you control the Test. Take the Test in order and it has a high probability of controlling you. So you get to decide how you want to do it. I tell them that I better not find out that you took the Test in order. It is a meaningless threat because there is nothing I can do to actually make them take the Test out of order. Many times somebody has not passed by 1 to 3 questions and they most always admit that they should have taken the Test out of order. Only one student has ever argued with me that taking the test out of order wouldn't work, then he did it his own way and didn't pass. Go figure.

The key to conquering overwhelm is making them practice flipping through the packets by categories. If that is what you want them to do on Test day, then make them do it that way while practicing in class. You will increase the chances that they will go out of order on Test day.

Affirmation: I am a genius and I apply my wisdom.

26

BREAKING THE FATIGUE SYNDROME

When we leave town to visit our relatives in New Mexico we drive 500 miles one way. Sitting in a car that long wears me out. I'm ready to go to bed when we get there. My wife sleeps as much as possible in the car, so she's ready to visit way into the night. Fatigue will set in when we sit too long.

How can we keep fatigue from happening when taking a 4 hour state assessment test? Actually, it is easy. Do not stay in your desk for longer than a half hour. What I tell my students to do is take breaks. Do the first category, which is the graphs, close your packet and get up. Ask to go to the bathroom. Sharpen your pencil. Ask the proctor to reset your calculator. Get out of your desk after 30 minutes and move around some!

One of my students brought a note from his mom that said if he got a leg cramp during the Test to please let him walk it off in the hallway, then he got a leg cramp after every category. The hall monitors were watching him like hawks out in the halls, trying to figure out what he was really doing. They never figured it out.

One kid went to the bathroom 9 times. He didn't need to go, he was just getting out of the room. The 2nd time he asked to go he was told no, because he had already gone. So he whispered the two magic words, *bladder infection,* and wound up going to the restroom 9 times. The point is to get out of your desk between categories. Move around some, take plenty of breaks and you will stop fatigue in it's tracks.

One of my students claimed she passed the state test

because she took 3 naps. Another girl put her head on her desk and was told to sit up by the proctor. The proctor had made it very plain if there were any irregularities during the Test that an Irregularity Report Form would be filled out, with dire consequences. My student said to the proctor; "You are interfering with the process I am using to take this Test, would you please bring the Irregularity Report Form because we must fill it out now!" It was like magic. The proctor did not bother her any more.

The students feel empowered when they take the Test using this process. It puts them in control. They like being in control. We do too. They work the problems out of numerical order and take their breaks. When the Test is over they feel great and are not as fatigued.

Just before they take their break, I have them check their running total for questions that they know they have right for sure. Fifty-three is the magic number to reach Commended Performance. This is a great motivational piece of the process. They always know where they are because they are keeping tally marks each time they know one is right.

The kid who went to the bathroom 9 times said he got 59 out of 60 correct for an almost perfect paper. He was bouncing off the walls. He was a special education kid with a long list of modifications and had never passed a State Assessment Math Test. His mother who worked in our building was at my door the afternoon of the Test, at the last bell. She wanted to know what I had done to her son because he was so wired, saying he got 59 of 60 correct because he went to the bathroom 9 times. I couldn't control myself as I burst out laughing, which made her laugh, too. After we were able to stop laughing and I explained to her the process we were using, she understood where he was coming from and was proud of him. I was skeptical that he had really gotten 59 right, but when the grades came back I was wrong.

Train your students to stop fatigue by taking little breaks. Fatigue will stop, they will stay fresh and score really high. It's already been proven.

Affirmation: I am a genius and I apply my wisdom.

27

JACKIE SCHOOLS THE DEPARTMENT CHAIR

I had just parked my car and headed into the building one day when Jackie said Hi! I asked her how she was getting along and she said great, but that she missed being in my class. I was her Algebra 2 teacher her junior year.

She said she wanted to thank me. She said that I was the reason she had passed the State Exit Math exam the year before, which is a graduation requirement. I said no you passed it yourself. She said that thanks to me she had finally passed that test and that she had failed the math test every year prior to her junior year.

I did not know she had never passed any of the prior state math tests. Well good then! She had overcome whatever had happened on all the prior tests.

A few days later, my department chair asked me what I had been doing to get everyone to pass the exit math test. I told him that once the students conquered overwhelm, fatigue and lack of confidence that they all soared.

He did not believe it. He wanted to see the curriculum I used as he was thinking that the curriculum was key. I told him the material was not the key. He asked to talk to some of my students. I set up a meeting and sent Jackie.

The department chair brought the master teacher and a curriculum person from the central office. They looked like a panel about to perform an inquisition, desks all lined up straight, one single chair in front of them for Jackie. She was about to blow their minds.

They asked her to explain how she had aced the state math test when she had never passed one before. One little sweet high school senior against three seasoned educators. She outnumbered them and set them all straight. It was amazing to watch.

They asked her what curriculum did the trick for her, that caused her to pass. She said she knew the entire curriculum already and just practicing it more was boring and was not what helped her pass.

She explained that taking the test out of order by categories kept her from bogging down and getting overwhelmed. She told them she took a break and left the room after each category to keep from getting fatigued. She said her confidence was sky high because she knew that after the first three categories she had passed and all the rest was just pushing her towards commended performance.

She added that she had used the same strategy on the science test too, by doing 3 categories, biology, chemistry and life science. She tried to break apart the English exam, but said it was not possible.

She proved my point that overwhelm, fatigue and confidence are some of the key factors on the state exams. Taking the test this way put her in complete control of the test, instead of the test controlling her.

They asked our entire math department to use the same method and strategy that year. Our school passing rate went up big time. The next year they returned to curriculum is key and the grades dropped. Hmm, let's discard what we know empowers the students and go back to what justifies some jobs in the curriculum office.

Whatever.

Just my suggestion, but when you find something that you can make work that empowers students to succeed, do it forever. My hunch is that it will all be about the process used and not just the curriculum by itself. Teach the curriculum and teach the process. Do both.

Affirmation: I am a genius and I apply my wisdom.

28

REQUISITE VARIETY

I took a 14 year vacation in the middle of my teaching career. After teaching for 7 years, I became the minister of a church in Elgin, Texas. I changed career's again for health insurance reasons due to our newborn son needing a kidney transplant and eventually took another ministry job in Terrell, Texas. This is where I became acquainted with NEURO LINGUISTIC PROGRAMMING. After completing NLP Practitioner, Master Practitioner, Trainer Training, Maximum Performance Technology, Time Line Therapy Practitioner and Master Practitioner, I returned to the math classroom after an absence of 14 years.

I had been successful as a classroom teacher before and discovered on the first day back in the classroom that almost everything I had done in my former life as a classroom teacher had changed and I would need to re-invent myself.

Of course, I should have known and expected things to be different. The students were different, the culture was different, I was different and education was different. Things are always changing.

After learning NLP, it occurred to me that perhaps I had changed the most. I was armed with lots of new techniques to practice. I could practice a new technique every day and place my focus, wherever I chose.

I had the feeling that I needed to unhinge my classroom. I was afraid to take my foot off the brake, so to speak, and open things up, thinking that I would not have control of things. Losing control of my classroom was the fear.

It took me a while to work up my nerve and take the hinges off. The practice routine was the first time I let it go. The thought of letting the kids get up, move around in class, and then wonder if I could ever get them back to work was my issue.

I was even more afraid of sending 16 kids to work the same problem on the big boards at the same time. What would happen? Would they work? Would it help them learn? Would they just goof around? How much copying of their neighbors work would they do? What might I learn from the exercise?

What I discovered was that my level of control increased by a huge margin! How could this be? I had, at the very least, 10 times more control than ever before. It was shocking! At the same time, it bordered on being really embarrassing.

For wanting to have so much control, I had to face the fact that the real reason that I had not had more control all the years prior was all because of me. If there was a scale from 1 to 10 for flexibility, I had been at 1 for some time.

Call it whatever you want, but as a group at times, school teachers are not really all that flexible. We like to do things the way we like to do things, and even the suggestion that we might try something new and improved is often met with derision.

If forced to choose between a staff development session or a root canal, many would pick the dentist chair, as the pain is less. (That's funny right there.)

Overall, we do not take too well to the idea that we are substandard. We might need to change some of our procedures, if change is actually necessary. We can be a hard group to teach.

Okay, so my wanting to keep control at all cost, had kept me from gaining 10 times as much control. Today it is more like 100 times.

The Law of Requisite Variety is responsible. It says that whoever is the most flexible will control the system. So if you want more control than you ever imagined you might ever have in your classroom, or anywhere else, become extremely flexible.

If you have been extremely rigid and have not had as much control as you would like, get flexible. This could be a stretch, this becoming extremely flexible. The change could be great, or not, depending on how flexible you become.

Now it's time for some ideas. Here are some of the ways I have taken my being so rigid to heart and how I am attempting to become extremely flexible.

1. The practice routine already described. One problem at a time, get up to have it graded for 100 points. Question #2 is worth 200 and so forth. Some of the kids were shocked when I had them add up their points at the end of class and they had 4500 points. Are you actually going to count all these, they wanted to know, of course, I said, you earned them. Kids up moving around, rowdiness going on while they were up, and thousands of points. Sounds like flexibility to me.

2. Sending 16 kids to the board at the same time to work the exact same problem. Lots of movement, talking and work. It also gives me the chance to stand behind them and watch to see where everybody is mathematically.

3. Ask students ahead of the curve to assist those who are not yet there. Listen to them explain things and compliment them. Okay, I admit some of them, at times, explain things better. Sometimes I have to correct them. All teachable moments. How many teachable moments might I have let pass me by in the past? Think about that one.

4. One year the assistant superintendent of secondary schools came to our math department meeting at the

beginning of school and said he wanted us to make our commended performance on the state assessment go up by 10%. This suggestion was met with a negative reaction from our entire department, including me. We discussed it at length after he left the room. Driving home that day it dawned on me that I had set the bar at passing for my students, which is definitely lower than earning commended performance. Why did I have a negative reaction to a suggestion to raise the expectation level? I wound up raising the level of what was expected and my commended performance numbers went up from 16% to 27%. Go figure.

I can't remember where I heard the story about two elementary teachers who each had 25 special education students. The principal told one teacher her kids were all special education that she had her work cut out for her. He then told the other one her kids were all gifted and talented and she had her work cut out for her. On the state assessment the kids who the teacher thought were gifted and talented scored way above the other class.

All of our kids are gifted and talented. If they don't know it yet, sounds like an opportunity for us.

Get rid of all your barriers to being the most flexible person in your building and become so flexible that you are willing to change any and everything to get the outcomes you are after.

You will have more control than you ever imagined. You'll also have tons more fun teaching. I know I do!

Affirmation: I am a genius and I apply my wisdom.

29

THE PRACTICE ROUTINE

The first year I taught math at RRHS I had three classes of Algebra 1 extended, as they called it. This was a class for historically low performers, which met every day, for three semesters. We were on a block, every other day schedule, so this was twice the classroom time as these classes were double blocked. No one wanted to teach Algebra 1 extended. The low performers can be hard to deal with, especially when grouped together. Learning how to deal with their attitudes took a ton of patience.

I began searching for anything that I could do to get them to do their work. It was immediately apparent that I could not assign them 20 problems to work on, as they would just close their books, thinking that it was time for social hour. It made me wonder if this is how they had gotten so far behind.

One day I decided to try a different approach and I offered them 100 points just for doing one problem. I gave them an easy equation to solve and told them to bring it up to me when they finished. They all did the question, brought their paper, I wrote either a 100 or a zero on it, it was a little rowdy to be sure, but the papers were all graded and they all went back to their desks. It worked good for one problem.

To get them to do the next problem, I offered them 200 points. They did it, brought their papers, 200 was written on it and it was rowdy again. It worked good on the second problem. All right.

I noticed on the third one, for 300 points, naturally, that

the room went from semi rowdy to as quiet as a funeral while they were working on the 3rd question. This was pretty interesting to watch. They turned all their attention to the problem. I mean all 100% of their attention was focused on the one problem in front of them. They did it, got their 300 points and sat back down. Pretty good on problem 3. So far so good.

So just how many would they do, before they shut it down? I decided to just keep going, why mess with what was working, right? They were working on the 22nd one when the bell rang to dismiss class. I had been watching the clock, but they had no idea how much time had elapsed as they were into it. They were sort of shocked when the bell rang. Where did the time go?

I said write your name on your papers, and turn them in. The next day I had them add up their point totals. With the last question being worth 2,200 points, the overall total was large. It was impressive to them that they had thousands of points. I let them watch me write these giant numbers in my grade book. Most of them just stared, with this really puzzling look. A couple asked if I was going to count those points and seemed almost shocked when I said, of course I was.

And so The Practice Routine was born. I set a goal to have them do between 20 and 30 problems in class per day. Most days were within that range. Their points added to some gigantic number that would not fit into the computer. Half their grade was their daily and homework average. Putting in a 100 for their daily work was much less than fair, actually, but I was constrained to that number.

On the first major test after The Practice Routine was introduced the grades took a big jump. It was evidence that they were learning and knew more about what they were doing.

We did The Practice Routine almost every day for the rest of the year. I would move to the next logical piece of Algebra 1, only after I was sure that they had really mastered the present one. Students that had never made good grades in a math class were now making A's and B's. This was more than shocking to them.

And every day by the 3rd or 4th problem, and for all that followed, it would again be as quiet as a funeral after the problem was written on the board, as they lost track of time. I was still working on just what was really happening. Why the silence? What was happening on the unconscious level? What was going on that would cause the total silence as well as the loss of time, when it had just been rowdy seconds before, as they were all up moving around the room?

Pavlov's dog came to mind. Okay, that was at the very least part of it. They had been trained and were just following the system, so to speak, but it didn't explain the silence and loss of time.

I knew as we discussed in a previous chapter that Pattern Interrupt had to be occurring. You could see that their old pattern of not success was no longer running. Their work was really all the evidence needed to prove Pattern Interrupt had happened. The old pattern of not being successful was gone. They were mastering their work.

I also knew that they were using what had to be a new strategy for them. Their Convincer Strategy became full, so they were now convinced that they could be successful. So they had just adapted a new strategy and left the old unsuccessful one behind, and were learning at a rapid pace. They weren't complaining about it either, which was refreshing to me.

Pavlov, check, Pattern Interrupt, check, Convincer Strategy, check, New Strategy, check, and still none of them explained the silence or the loss of time. What else was happening that would account for a trance so strong that they lost track of time? I wonder?

Affirmation: I am a genius and I apply my wisdom.

30

FRACTIONATION

The Psychological Phenomenon called FRACTIONATION is working in the real world! Seriously? Years ago, I developed the practice routine described in the last chapter. The goal of the routine was to get the kids to work the entire 90 minute period. I already confessed to being idealistic, so stop bugging me about it! Okay?

I would give them a problem to solve and they would bring me their paper for grading. It gets rowdy with all of them up moving around. I would put the next problem on the screen and repeat the process. We would do as many as 25 rounds some days, depending on how many issues they were having and the degree of difficulty of the topic.

I started noticing that on about the 4th or 5th question the room would go from loud and rowdy to totally quiet, hear a pin drop, totally silent. The first time I noticed it, I thought, "Oh that's nice", as it was much too noisy to suit me. Then on all successive problems when the next problem went on the screen, total silence would follow.

This went on 3 periods a day, 3 or 4 times a week. Eventually my curiosity got the best of me and I had to know what was really going on? What could explain the silence? I began paying more attention to it, to see if I could explain what was happening.

One day we were practicing along and the dismissal bell rang. None of us knew we were up against the end of the period! That perplexed me even more. Now I needed to explain the silence and that time had disappeared. It is not normal in a 90 minute class for teenagers to get so engrossed in what they are working on for time to slip away and disappear and no one be aware that the bell is about to ring. Time had disappeared for me, too.

Actually, the time part of this seemed somewhat common to me, as I could recount numerous occasions when I would be working on something and get so absorbed, that when I did finally look at the clock, I would be amazed that so much time had passed.

I love the movie Dances With Wolves! I remember when we saw it in the theater that I did not want it to end and actually thought my watch was broken when the movie ended because it did not seem like a 3 hour movie. It is a 3 hour movie and I was totally into it, so time disappeared.

I had just never seen this phenomenon happening in an Algebra class, of all places. So I became extremely curious about this loss of time. What would explain it? Did an explanation even exist? The fact that the time loss was happening almost every day sent me on a quest, searching for an explanation.

Total silence was occurring and time was disappearing beginning on the 4th or 5th problem, each day. The days were passing fast. The students were learning. I knew where each one was because I was looking at their work 20 or more times per day. I was having a blast. Their confidence was growing. Their grades were rising on tests. All was going great and I was perplexed to know what was really happening. I continued my quest, searching for the explanation and stumbled onto it about 3 weeks later.

It is the psychological phenomenon called FRACTIONATION. It does not have anything to do with math or a Nation of Fractions. It is all about the changing of states. I do not mean going from Texas to Oklahoma, as this changing of states is psychological.

I was changing the students from one state to another, multiple times each day. The first state was one of concentration, as they would work an algebra problem. The second state is actually what the experts refer to as, "breaking state", as they would come out of their state of concentration and get up to have the problem graded.

On the next problem they would go back into their state of concentration, come out for the grading, back in, then out, etc. In, out, in, out, in, out, in, out, and after the 4th or 5th cycle the silence and the disappearance of time would begin to show up. I had just been shifting their states back and forth. All right, I can live with that.

I had been FRACTIONATING them. I had heard of this phenomenon before and I began to suspect I had unconsciously devised the Practice Routine to take advantage of it. Okay, I do a lot of things unconsciously and so do you. As teachers we do a lot of things by instinct, most of us say, and really it is just our unconscious minds at work.

Hypnotherapists most often use FRACTIONATION. They understand how it works and have been trained to use it. They know that all change really happens unconsciously. So does all learning. If you really know it, you can pull it up when you need it, right? Most of my math teacher colleagues say that after they have taught a course for 4 or 5 years, they go on automatic pilot with the material. They mean that they really just have it loaded on their internal hard drive, or their unconscious mind.

The way the hypnotherapist uses fractionation is to get the client to shift into an unconscious state. They use a set of skills that allow them to talk to the unconscious. The clients conscious mind will interrupt and get in the way and the client will come out into a conscious state and the therapist will get them to go unconscious again knowing that when they do they will automatically go twice as deep unconsciously as they were the first time.

Then the conscious mind will interrupt again, and when they go unconscious again, they go twice as deep again, and on and on it goes. After about 4 or 5 times going twice as deep, shifting from unconscious to conscious and back, they get far enough down in their unconscious that they will just stay there, which is where the real changes they are seeking will take place.

The unconscious is not aware of time like the conscious mind. The unconscious is always awake, which explains why some of the best ideas you ever had came while your conscious mind was asleep. Of course, because your conscious mind was not awake to interrupt. Cool.

I had my explanation. The reason it was getting quiet after the 4th or 5th round in Algebra class was because they had gone twice as deep unconsciously, 4 or 5 times. The same thing was true for the loss of time. Once they had gone unconscious, their conscious mind (time keeper) was silent, so time effectively had disappeared.

Back in the chapter when they were using a new process to make commended performance on the state assessment, they were working a category for 20 to 30 minutes, taking a break outside the room, when they came back they were going twice as deep in their state of concentration, taking another break, going twice as deep again, in, out, in, out, etc. In essence, their unconscious mind was taking the test. The unconscious mind always makes a higher grade. It's where all the learning is stored. They would make comments like, "The longer I worked, the easier it got!" What an interesting description of fractionation at work.

This is pretty wild, right? Yes it is, although I would say very powerful.

What a picture it is to behold, empowered students, using their brains in such a way, to access all prior knowledge, all while keeping the conscious mind from messing things up. Yippy Skippy!

After tracking my data for a few years, the students that took control of the state test the way I taught them to, consistently had 10 more questions answered correctly compared to our schools average. Our schools average stayed at about 82% and the empowered student's average stayed at about 97%. Of course!

Could it really be any other way, since it is your unconscious mind that is taking the test? Not a chance.

So, think of how many different ways you might get your students to shift from one state to another, and then back again, etc. Come up with how you could use fractionation in the subject you teach. Watch for both the loss of time and the silence.

I wonder if fractionation could be performed when making a public speech. Absolutely! It can! Shift the audience from a serious state to a funny state, back into seriousness, out for funny, etc. It is fun to do and naturally a point in time will occur when the audience becomes absolutely totally still, unconscious, so to speak. So watch for it. I often see this happen when I'm speaking at church. What a trip! You should give it a whirl.

Affirmation: I am a genius and I apply my wisdom.

31

HOW TO PRESENT AN EFFECTIVE LESSON

The short answer is, Practice, Practice, Practice, naturally. However, nothing makes up for effective training about what you should really be doing. After training at a School of Theology, I was under the mistaken impression that I was fully prepared for making public speeches. Theologically perhaps, I was prepared. Presentation wise I was not.

At the first church where I served, occasionally I would notice during my Sunday morning lesson, that the audience would be transfixed, hypnotized as it were, which is much better than me putting them all to sleep. (Ha!) I was aware when this phenomenon would occur, but had no idea why or how it happened, if I was causing it, or not, if it was just by chance, or when, if ever, it would happen again. Sometimes it would happen, sometimes it didn't. It seemed random.

Then one Wednesday I went to the weekly downtown Kiwanis meeting, and the guest speaker was a psychologist who specialized in hypnotherapy. He held the audience transfixed as we were all hanging on every word. I asked him what he had done after the meeting; he laughed and said something like "trade secrets can't be divulged." He had done whatever he had done on purpose, but what had he actually done? The "hanging on every word" was the same phenomenon that I would see, every now and then, randomly speaking, while I was speaking at church.

So with my eyes opened to the possibilities, and my curiosity at an all time high, I embarked on the journey that would change my life. The quest was to learn how to have them "hanging on every word", each and every time.

My world changed, my life changed, it was fun, it was very challenging, it has taken lots of work and practice, and all because I decided to delve into the world of speaking to the unconscious mind. As I discovered, there is a whole set of skills to communicate with the unconscious mind. Go figure. These skills were not taught in Homiletics 101 or in Speech for Secondary Teachers.

The last time I spoke at my former church (I was not on staff), when the worship leader announced that I would be speaking that morning, some in the church applauded. Although it was a little embarrassing, it is nice to be liked. I understood this was really feedback. I would much rather have them react that way than dead silence or hissing. (Ha!)

And more importantly, what it meant was that the group rapport skills I had sought to build had been successful and that a former lesson had connected with them. I interpreted the applause as not only had "they liked it", but that my attempt to establish unconscious rapport with the audience had worked to some degree.

Sensory acuity can tell you many things. Where are they? Do they have this? Can I go on? How much, if any, do I need to stall to allow their minds to catch up? Am I going too fast, too slow, did I lose them, etc? Read the audience. What did you just read? What must be done based on what you just read?

Since there is no failure, only feedback, a new task of mine might be called feedback sorting. What does the feedback mean? What has to be true in the other person's model of the world, for them to be giving you feedback, whatever the feedback is?

It was fairly common at my former church for me to get some feedback about one of my prior lessons. This is a little strange because I only speak there a couple of times a year. I just fill in sometimes when the pastor is away. And yet, I would get some feedback almost every Sunday.

I believe that this happens because rapport on the unconscious level is a very powerful tool. It is also uncommon. Most people do not have much experience with someone speaking to their unconscious mind. They really like it, though.

They do not know what it really is that I am doing, but they know that I know what it is. Therefore, their curiosity draws them to talk to me. They will talk about a lesson I did back in the past sometime, just like they had just heard it. The feedback is that the lesson went onto their hard drive, so to speak. They have it on the unconscious level. God's truth got past the guard at the door of their mind and was processed on the inside. Powerful stuff.

This process of speaking to the unconscious mind has become one giant learning experience for me, as the curiosity and learning continue at a rapid rate. For example, I was not aware of the cumulative effect of speaking to the unconscious mind, at first.

However, I learned that the effort and energy spent building rapport on the unconscious level tends to stockpile. The next time you speak, no one who has heard you before starts at zero, on the unconscious rapport meter. They are curious to hear you again.

This is great. The task of building unconscious rapport with the entire audience just got much easier. I know what you're wondering, and you are right, there is a whole set of group unconscious rapport building skills, aren't there? Yes. They are all on the unconscious level, of course.

Actually, there are many skills in the set of skills of speaking to the unconscious mind and rapport building is just one of them. When Dr. Dan first told us everything that he wanted us to do in a presentation I was overwhelmed. Each facet seemed like it was too much, just by itself. Just how was I going to do over a dozen of them at the same time?

That's right, practice, practice, practice.

The journey has been exciting. I prayed that God would help me find a place to be trained. He sent a new couple to our church that had taken all the trainings that I was interested in taking. They introduced me to Dr. Dan and his wife Linda, who are fantastic trainers. After few years, I had been certified in all 5 levels of NLP.

The skills set I was taught all come from Neuro Linguistic Programming. (NLP) The International Neuro Linguistic Programming Trainers Association (INLPTA) has very high standards, trains internationally, and has certifications in 3 major areas. 1. NLP Practitioner, 2. NLP Master Practitioner, and 3. NLP Trainer Training.

I have been certified as an NLP Practitioner, NLP Master Practitioner, NLP Business Trainer, Time Line Therapy Practitioner, Time Line Therapy Master Practitioner, and Maximum Performance Technology Practitioner.

So, my suggestion "How to present an Effective Lesson" is that it takes a lot of work. If you are interested in being an effective communicator get all the training you can get. There are lots of great schools who can teach you great content. Then INLPTA can teach you how to present it in a powerful way.

And for those interested in speaking the Word of God, always remember how powerful it is, that He will indwell you as you speak, and in turn fill the hearts of all who hear.

Affirmation: I am a genius and I apply my wisdom.

32

NESTED LOOPS

Loop 1

I have a very good friend, David, who is a chemical engineer. He is brilliant. Early in his career he was the new hire, young engineer, starting off on his first job at a large gulf coast refinery. His first assignment was to go assess the major problems that were happening at one of the units at the refinery.

He had no idea how to fix anything. He said he would give it a shot and went to work. A few weeks later he presented a plan to correct all the problems and his superiors were very impressed. All his plans were enacted and all the problems disappeared. Just like that problems that had existed for years were solved.

He became known as Mr. Fix It. He really had no clue how to fix anything, according to him, but, with his new unofficial title of Mr. Fix It, he was worried, because what he suspected would happen happened.

That's right, they gave him other impossible problems to fix, and he fixed them, too. He fixed problem after problem. He was Mr. Fix It.

I know that right now you are thinking that there is some kind of catch or trick to all this, right? No tricks. This is a true story. The guy just out of college with no experience was fixing everything. He started getting promoted.

He has been flown all over the world to fix problems in refineries. According to him he has used the same technique all these years. It has worked time and time again. Experience has also been a good teacher. He has grown, of course, and today is recognized as an industry expert. He can fix anything, whether it is in a refinery, or not.

Today he is more like an organizational expert than he is a chemical engineer, as he has fixed more companies than just refineries. If you need an organization fixed and are really willing to do whatever it would take, changing whatever really needed changing, he would be the man to call.

Would you believe that the way he has fixed all kinds of companies over the past 40 years is an extremely easy process? Sound crazy, right? To think that a man with no experience when he began could fix so many things. I know. It is pretty wild.

The one thing I know for sure is that my life would not be what it is today if I had not met Mr. Fix It. Everyone needs a friend like him. He always speaks the truth. He commands unbelievable respect. Little kids love him instantly, too, which has always been amazing to watch.

So what he has done all these years is part of the secret, I believe, to saving our educational system. You are probably eager for me to quit stalling and just go ahead and get it out there, aren't you? I will in just a minute.

I need to tell you a story first, okay?

Loop 2

There is a school district down by Houston that had had falling TAKS scores over the past several years. The ratings had been very low. So, they hired a consultant to help them. He began his investigation to find out what was really wrong and what needed to be done about it.

The answer he found was surprising to the school board. They accepted all of his recommendations. Within 3 years all their schools had taken a huge jump in all the ratings, many becoming recognized or exemplary.

The change was remarkable. Groups from all over the USA began coming to visit in their never ending search to find educational utopia. Surely they had found the missing link. So just how did they make such a big turn so fast?

The answer is easy. It was not popular, however, with some, as changing was required. Part of the problem was the unwillingness to change. A second one was that the right things had to be changed. The things that the consultant had them change were the right things. Therefore, things changed.

So, if you want to fix anything, and you are not willing to change what really needs changing, you would wind up spinning your wheels.

What they changed was popular with some and unpopular with others, but it worked. There is something here for all of us educators to learn. Change always comes with a cost. They were willing to change, so they did, and now they are being viewed as doing the impossible.

What they actually did was pretty easy. It has made me consider applying to teach there, which my wife said was okay with her, then she mentioned that the drive home every night would be a killer. She got me on that one, smart girl.

Therefore, before I tell you what they did, I direct you to think about the concept that Dr. Steven Covey, as well as many before and after him like to talk about. It goes like this, "IF YOU KEEP ON DOING WHAT YOU'VE ALWAYS DONE YOU'LL KEEP ON GETTING WHAT YOU'VE ALWAYS GOTTEN". Or sometimes they say it this way, "Insanity is doing things the same old way you've always done them while expecting a different result."

Be patient for a second and I'll tell you what they did, but, first I need to tell you another story.

Loop 3.

In Statistics we have a topic that is called Hypothesis Testing. So what happens in Hypothesis Testing? I knew you were thinking that. If you guessed that a Hypothesis is Tested you would be right.

The Hypothesis Tested could be any idea, it could be to see how effective a new drug is, a program installed to solve some problem, or anything else that can be tested. So, we test hypotheses.

What is interesting is that from experience there are two common errors that can occur. These are called Type I and Type II errors. All kinds of entities, public and private are guilty of committing one, or sometimes both errors. There is usually no rush to admit this, naturally, for a variety of reasons. The tendency is to spin them, which only compounds the effect of the errors.

I knew you would be interested in these two common errors and just how they would apply to the world of education. I admit to making both errors in the past. You may have made them as well. Just what we do to prevent them is really not all that tough. All you have to do is be blatantly honest.

Go figure. You personally can avoid these errors by being honest. Being honest is only difficult if we have blinders on or are not interested in facing the truth. Being honest and facing the truth leads to the avoidance of both Type I and Type II errors.

So, there is the 3rd loop. The two types of errors in Hypotheses Testing. I'll tell you what they are soon, as I must discuss the 3 nested loops I have been setting up, for the purpose that you can both learn and experience nested loops.

Nested Loops.

By definition a nested loop is something that is not finished. The ending is left dangling. To illustrate nested loops, I began talking about my friend David, the school district in Houston and the two types of errors made in hypothesis testing.

Think about the last novel you read. The writer will get to the end of a chapter and leave someone in trouble. The next chapter will shift to a different context. They are masters at using nested loops.

Screen writers do much the same thing. They will introduce something that opens the loop, and then later in the movie they provide the answer, which closes the loop.

The use of Nested Loops is a powerful tool. On the unconscious level what happens when a Nested Loop is opened is that the conscious mind will sort through all kinds of possible endings. By the time 3 or more loops are opened the conscious mind will be very busy working on all the possible scenarios, so then is the best time to talk straight to the unconscious mind. The conscious mind is busy. It will most likely leave you alone.

I have found that speaking at church is a much easier setting to use nested loops than in math class. In class if I want to use a loop I will start a joke and then hold the punch line until later. At church I will start 3 stories and not end them, until after the first part of all three are told.

By the time I have the 3 loops set the audience is most often totally focused on what I am doing. The Bible study part of the lesson comes next with the intention that the message goes right onto their unconscious hard drive, so to speak.

Then the loops are to be closed in reverse order. Lay them out 1,2,3 and close them 3,2,1. Then I am done and I stop.

The lesson always seems very fast to me. Time flies for both the audience and me.

That's how I use nested loops. If you teach history you

might want to play with some with Nested Loops. Give them a try and see how it goes. Just practice.

You can listen to me using them on line at hpf.org if you like. Lessons that I presented will be listed under, sermons, archive, and them look for my name. I use three Nested Loops every time.

Closing Loop #3. Type 1 and Type 2 Errors

A Type I error is when you set forth an idea or program, and then declare it a smashing success when the statistics say that nothing changed. Politicians are famous at the Type I error. In our world of education we can make it too if we are not careful. For example, a new process for getting the kids to pass the STATE Tests can be declared a smashing success, when the statistical data actually shows that nothing changed from the prior year. We then might rationalize the results by saying that we all know that our scores would have fallen dramatically had we not instituted the new study program. You might want to closely watch all conclusions as it is extremely easy to make a Type I error.

The Type II error works in reverse. We stop doing something that we say didn't work, when the statistical data shows that it actually did work. For example, when President Reagan instituted massive cut in taxes in the early 1980's, the net effect was that millions of jobs were created, mostly by small business owners who used all the money that had been going to taxes to grow their businesses. All the people that they hired wound up paying more overall tax than if the business owners had just had their taxes raised and did not grow their businesses. The overall amount of taxes raised was staggering.

Somewhere in there the decision was made to stop the tax breaks. They made the Type II error. They said it wasn't working and stopped doing it, when it was really working.

They did this because of politics not reason. Who gets the credit is what drives the politicians, along with making sure they get re-elected. They also knew it worked.

This seems very easy to me. If something does not work, quit doing it. If something works, keep doing it. Duh.

Closing Loop #2 The Houston Area School District

So here, in so many words, is what the consultant told them. It was a fact that they had been hiring a new superintendent about every 3 years, which meant that they were being used by these guys to get a bigger, better, more high paying job somewhere else.

During the 3 years that they were there they would install their pet system and just about the time the teachers in their district got it down the new guy would come in and they would start all over with the next pet system. Fifteen years later they had been changed to death, so to speak.

So the consultant told them to figure out what they wanted and to require the next superintendent to manage that and kill the pet system routine. The board was willing to do this, only coming up with what they really wanted seemed like a daunting challenge. So why not use the experts that already work for you, that have the day to day interface with the students?

This seemed logical to the board. So this little project was turned over to the teachers. They designed the system to be used. They put it in place. They had both the power and the responsibility to implement it, and so they did.

Within two years their schools had succeeded in becoming acceptable, or recognized and in some cases exemplary. Schools boards began flying in from all over the country to see what new fantastic thing had been discovered in the never ending search for educational utopia.

The new superintendent was told to manage the system

and was not given the power to change it, in any way. If he tried he would be fired, so they said. They hired him to manage and not implement his own theories.

Sound too easy? In a way it is, because, that's how empowerment works. In this case, they empowered their faculty. The truth is that to adopt the new superintendent's model of education has always been a tough sell for the faculty. Buy in is hard to get. Here we go again with another pet system. I worked for RRISD for 19 years and we did 6 pet systems.

Close Loop #1. David's secret.

David had no clue how to solve all these serious problems at the refinery. So he interviewed everyone who was directly involved at the unit in question and asked them what they would do to solve the problem. His plan consisted of everything they told him to do.

When he presented it to his superiors, which included the refinery CEO, he did not tell them where he got the ideas, because of the huge disconnect that existed between management and labor. They didn't trust each other. So, he kept that part quiet. He became Mr. Fix It.

We would all be better off if we were more interested in doing what is in the best interest of the students than protecting our own turf, justifying the existence of our jobs and climbing the ladder.

The question we don't want to answer is this: "HOW IS IT POSSIBLE THAT WE HAVE NOT ALREADY FIXED EVERYTHING THAT IS WRONG WITH EDUCATION"?

Deep down you know the answer. Me too. Since the only person you can change is you, when your door closes each day and class begins, do everything you would want to be done by every teacher that is teaching your own children. Do everything you would want a teacher to do for you if you were in their class.

Affirmation: I am a genius and I apply my wisdom.

33

SENSORY ACUITY

Sensory Acuity is what you see, hear and feel!

The experts tell us that the percentages for words, sounds, and physical queues are roughly 7%, 38% and 55%. This means that the words only count for 7%, the smallest of all. As teachers it is only natural for us to think that words are king. We present lessons, we make sure we say it right, the content is so important to us; we revel in it, and even like to say we "know our stuff".

And yet it only counts for 7% of our communication. Hmm... maybe we haven't been spending enough time paying attention to the other 93%, right? Right! We have no doubt missed lots of clues, to what is really going on by just focusing on the words being used.

After my blinders had been removed, I knew I had a lot of ground to make up and needed to find as many ways as possible to track the other 93% of communication.

I am auditory by nature so the 38% of sound, which includes tone and timbre, was easier for me than the physical ques. The tone of voice is often more telling than the actual words themselves. If the tone is rude, that will be the message that is received, regardless of the actual words. The actual words will get discounted because the rudeness will become a roadblock. "He was just rude"!! "What did he actually say?" Often there is no clue to what was said, as it doesn't matter because they had already tuned us out. We are often times kind, with our tone of voice. We might be loud and kind, or soft and kind, though soft and kind will get us farther. It is simply more inviting. Some of us have one volume, loud, or very loud, or soft, or so soft it can't be heard. We all know people that vary their pitch for effect.

I have found that a whisper, at times, will bring the whole class to attention. Try it and see what happens. When I get to teaching real fast it is always louder. When they tell me to slow down, I get softer.

They can tell if you love them, or not, by your tone. What is your tone like to them? What do you think they would say? If they said boring, about my tone, it would be like a slap in the face! I would never want to be boring.

The truth hurts sometimes, and sometimes the truth is that our tone tells on us! It tells them we are passionate about our subject, or it may tell them that we really don't want to be here. Our tone might tell our students that we are mad and don't mess with me today. Our tone can say anything: sad, angry, stressed, bored, afraid, frustrated, passionate, focused, excited, bland, tired, sick, you name it. All can be communicated just with our tone. 38% trumps 7%, meaning your tone of voice is 5 times more powerful than your words.

What message would you like to be sending your students every day when they walk into your room? Either your tone of voice has been communicating that message or it hasn't! The tone that I have learned to get the most out of is the one that communicates fun and excitement. My tone says I am having fun! What could possibly be more fun than math, right?

When you look back to your years in school, did you ever have a teacher that hated the subject that they were teaching? You know, like a math teacher that hated math! Or a history teacher that can't keep WW1 and WW2 events straight! An English teacher that uses bad grammar! Our students read us like a book. What does the book we are presenting with our tone say to them?

Okay, we got it, maybe our tone of voice needs some work. Right, 5 times more than our words do!

And now for the top dog, big cheese, big boss, chief of chiefs! Our physical ques comprise 55% of our communication.

Physical Queues:

Hands: what are they doing? Are they: folded, fidgeting, active, passive, what are the fingers doing, the thumbs?

Head: nodding, still, saying no or saying yes.

Eyes: What are the eyes doing? Where are they looking? What message are they communicating.

When you are teaching what are you doing with your hands? Feet? Legs? Arms? Head? Are these ques congruent with your words? Watch this one carefully. If your words are saying yes, but your head is going back and forth saying no, you are not congruent. They will not believe what you are saying. Why should they, if you don't believe it why should they believe it?

Virginia Satir came up with some methods years ago to send your message based on what you are doing with your arms and hands. There are 5 of them.

1. Thinker: When the speaker puts one hand on his chin, it's the classic thinker pose.
2. Blamer: When one hand is on a hip and the other one is pointing and shaking an index finger, it's the classic blamer pose.
3. Leveler: When arms are horizontal with palms down it's the classic level pose, which has the effect of calming your audience.
4. Placater: When the arms are horizontal with the palms up, it's the classic placate pose, which says please go with me on this.

5. Distracter: When the arms are extended and flying everywhere it's the classic distracter pose, which has the effect of communicating fun.

It's worth the effort to study Virginia Satir, if you like. Her work has helped me in the adjustments of my tone of voice and physical queues.

Affirmation: I am a genius and I apply my wisdom.

34

WYATT RIPS ME

I had a big presentation to make in NLP Trainer Training. I was nervous. I had worked on it hard. The author of *TIME LINE THERAPY AND THE BASIS OF PERSONALITY,* Wyatt Woodsmall, would be in the audience. After each presentation was made that day it would be feedback time.

Dr. Dan would ask what you thought about what you had just presented, what you would change if you did it again, etc. Then the members of the audience would take a few minutes to provide high level sensory feedback. Woodsmall would be offering his feedback, too. What would he say?

After everyone had provided me with some feedback, it was Woodsmall's turn. He had insisted on going last. Well, he said, and launched into a 10 minute rebuke of everything wrong with my presentation. You could have left them hanging with the basketball story you told, but of course you didn't! Instead of saying it the right way, which would have been to say, "the ball bounce off the rim, hit the backboard, and then,......", you could have left them hanging that way, but you ruined the effect by not dragging it out. I know you know how to do this, but you didn't. On and on he went ripping me apart.

It was devastating and humiliating to endure his feedback. The truth was that he was right on every point. My presentation had been a disaster. It was helpful to hear his feedback. I had taken it as a rebuke, when it was really just feedback. It remains the single most important presentation

I have ever made, due to the fact that I was forced to grow past my mistakes and make progress.

Dr. Dan called me a couple of weeks later as we were working on a project together. At the end of the call I said something to him about Woodsmall's feedback and my devastation. He said he hadn't noticed anything out of the ordinary about the feedback. Two days later he called me back and said I needed to come to Dallas and make my presentation again. I didn't see this coming, but agreed. Two weeks later I redid it and nailed it.

It is the only time I have ever seen Wyatt Woodsmall. I most likely will never see him again. He changed my public speaking in a huge and dramatic way. I am so thankful for being put through the ringer, so to speak.

We all need people to tell us the truth about what we do. Forget the sugar coated version. They can see things that we cannot. We need them to tell us the uncensored version. This is almost impossible at the school where you work. Could we really separate their intention from the idea they are trying to run us off? Probably not!

We can all be better at everything we do. We have no problem telling our students what they need to change to make progress. Who do you have that will tell you the truth, the whole truth and nothing but the truth? Would you even be able to accept it from them? Would you ever make real progress without the feedback? Perhaps not!

You may not be able to get that kind of feedback at your school. Find somewhere where you can. If it is not at work, they will not be after your job, but will tell you the truth and it will help you grow. You always want to make progress. You have to have the real unvarnished feedback to make progress. Go for it! Accept what they tell you. Change everything you can. Blossom where you are.

Affirmation: I am a genius and I apply my wisdom.

35

RADIANS: WHY DON'T THEY THINK THEY ARE EASY?

I did not say anything at the time during our last Pre-Calculus meeting, but something began to gnaw at me. My problem was that like the rest of the group, I knew that getting the students to understand radians in trigonometry seemed to be a big stretch. Angles can be measured in radians and in degrees. We use both in Trigonometry.

What was I doing or not doing to cause this lack of knowledge? I know that I can think in radians and my students cannot, yet. The lack of radian knowledge was not going to disappear on its own.

If I kept on doing what I had always done, my students were still going to be lacking in radian knowledge.

Therefore, I began thinking about what I wanted the students to think and do when they saw something like Cosecant 7 pi over 3. Bear with me here on the math.

First: Find the reference angle. It is pi over 3. Check. That seemed easy. Good job.

Second: I made a unit quarter circle of just quadrant 1 to emphasize the reference angle concept. Finding pi over 3 in quadrant 1, happened very fast. Check.

Three: Cosecant and Sine are reciprocals. Check. I knew that.

Four: So, read the Sine from pi over 3 in quadrant 1. It is the Y value, which is root 3 over 2. Check.

Five: Take the reciprocal of Sine. It is 2 over root 3. Rationalized, if you have them rationalize it is 2 root 3 over 3.

Check.

Six: The answer is either positive 2 root 3 over 3, or it's negative 2 root 3 over 3. Check. But which one is it?

Seven: Find out which quadrant 7 pi over 3 is in. How do you do that? You can do it the slow way or the fast way, take your pick. The slow way is on the calculator, the fast way is in your head.

Slow way: Change 7 pi over 3 into a decimal. Check. Draw a circle with X and Y axis'. Label only 0, pi over 2, pi, 3 pi over 2 and 2 pi, all the points on an axis of your unit circle. Changing them into decimals they become 0, 1.57, 3.14, 4.71. and 6.28. 7 pi over 3 is 7.237. Subtract 6.28, or 1 rotation. You get 1.05, which is between 0 and 1.57, so 7 pi over 3 is in quadrant one. The angle makes a full circular turn and stops in quadrant 1. Check. It only took the kids 20 seconds to do this the slow way on their calculator.

Fast way: 6 pi over 3 is the same as 2 pi if you reduce the fraction, which is one complete revolution. So you need one more pi over 3, to get to 7 pi over 3. The angle is in quadrant 1. Check. 5 seconds max for the fast way. It is at least 4 times faster.

Eight: All trig functions are positive in quadrant 1. Viola! The answer is positive 2 root 3 over 3.

Okay. So could the kids do this?

Yes, they could.

They said, "You just look at the denominator to determine the reference angle?" Yes. (Duh)

I had them do 5 or 6 problems this way on their little white boards, one at a time of course, holding up their answers for me to see. By the 4th one everyone in the room had caught up. They were losing their fear of radians. Check. Go figure. In the end they were just afraid of radians. No wonder they didn't think they were easy.

To test them I then had them find the Secant of 240

degrees. Some kid in the back of the room asked if it was okay if he changed the angle into radians first, then found the Secant. Knock yourself out. This was hilarious, as they usually want to change all the radian angles to degrees, then work the problem, then change the answer back to radians. He decided it was easier to find the reference angle if it was in radians, since it would just be the denominator. LOL.

The gnawing has stopped. Check.

Maybe the real issue was they did not understand what a reference angle was.

Maybe it was, maybe it wasn't.

Either way, they don't get a free pass on knowing how to use radians in my room. The more they use them the easier they get. Right!

Therefore, when any problem comes up that your students are struggling with in any class you teach, break it down as low as you can and figure out how to get them to do it. Whatever it takes, make sure they have the concept down before you go to the next one.

If you are not a math teacher, I most likely lost you with the Cosecant stuff. That's ok, but just get the fact that you can break down anything you teach into teeny tiny parts.

Break it down into the smallest pieces possible, so that it will be impossible to not succeed. Thanks again, Dr. Dan.

Affirmation: I am a genius and I apply my wisdom.

36

SMOKED BY SMOKER

Mr. Smoker was a retired military veteran. Seems like he was a drill Sargent in the marines, but perhaps he wasn't. He acted like he was by being tough, harsh and demanding. I was afraid of him, as was most of my class.

Early during the first week in Geometry class a kid talked back to Mr. Smoker. That was a big mistake. Mr. Smoker stomped over to the kid's desk, which just happened to be by the door and asked him what he had just said. The kid repeated it. Mr. Smoker picked the desk up with the kid still in it, turned towards the door and bowled the desk towards the open door. The desk scooted along the floor, through the door, crossed the hall and crashed into the coke machine. Nobody ever talked back to him again.

Later, when we got to the section where the Proofs began I was lost. The concept of doing a formal 2-column proof was too foreign. One day in class Mr. Smoker started a proof on the board, wrote the given information as step 1, walked to the back of the room and said, "Listen class as Mr. Massie tells us what the next step is on this proof!"

I had no clue and said: "I'm so sorry Mr. Smoker, sir, but I don't know the next step on this proof!" He huffed over, stood behind me, reached up his powerful hand and pinched the nerve on the top of my right shoulder with about a half grip and repeated, "I said, listen class as Mr. Massie tells us the next step on this proof!"

It hurt very badly. I said, half crying this time, "I am so sorry Mr. Smoker, sir, but I do not know the next step on this proof!" He then went from half grip to a full grip. Ouch! I looked at the board and thought that if I didn't figure out the next step really fast that I might actually die.

Somehow my brain saw every step and I told him the 2nd step, he released his grip a little, then the 3rd, 4th, 5th steps until the proof was finished. With each step he would release his a grip a little. Then he said, "I knew you could do it!"

Several things happened after this little episode. For starters, I never missed a step on any other proof. Since the first half of Geometry used to be about 70% proofs this was great for me. A second thing was that the fear level in our class escalated with everyone except me. I was no longer afraid of him, which seemed strange.

I still tell my Geometry students this story every year. They all want to know if I sued Mr. Smoker, if the police arrested him, what my parents said when they found out I had been abused and if the incident was on 60 minutes. I try to describe to them what school was like in the 1960's, to no avail. It was a different world.

They are also surprised when I say that I never told my parents. I didn't because I knew that they would have said, "Why didn't you just answer the question when he asked you the first time?"

Mr. Smoker was my favorite teacher in high school. He made me want to be a math teacher. I loved him! He was only at our school for 2 years. I still miss him and the impact he had on me. I only saw him once about 20 years after high school, which was great. I still use his phrase, "Listen class as Mr. Jones tells us the next step on this proof!" I don't pinch anyone, of course, but might ask later, if necessary, "Do I need to call Mr. Smoker and get him up here to help you with this proof?" It always gets a smile.

Looking back at my school days, I am thankful for all my teachers. Their impact on my life is everlasting. Please remember that you are making an everlasting impact on the lives of your students and that they will appreciate you most when they look back at their school days.

And you just had the thought didn't you, or not? Something is backwards, isn't it? You are right. Teachers are not always appreciated in the present, but more often than not our appreciation comes in the future when our students look back into their past and remember us.

Affirmation: I am a genius and I apply my wisdom.

37

LUNCH WITH THE AP'S

The cafeteria at our school was also the auditorium as there was a long stage on one side of the rectangular room. Mr. C and I ate lunch in the cafeteria for a few years and talked about sports.

He was a hockey fan and we both liked football and basketball, so we always had plenty of sports to talk about. We hardly paid any attention to what 600 students were doing while they were eating lunch.

Our Assistant Principals would most often be there too, depending on the events of the day, or they might be stuck in the office and running late to lunch.

The tables where we would all sit were up on the stage, which gave the impression that many eyes were watching the students. It was a good impression, but not true for Mr. C and I. We were engrossed in our favorite conversation.

Some days during the first lunch we would be the only adults in the cafeteria when lunch started. The AP's would come in as they could, sometimes on time, sometimes late and a few times none would get there at all. They all intended to show up on time. In a huge school like ours, it could not always happen. It all depended on what was happening on any given day.

Three things happened because we ate lunch on the stage every day.

First, we got to know all the AP's on a more personal level. It was interesting to hear them converse. We got a complete picture of what life was like for an AP. They get pulled and pushed from every direction imaginable, as they have a hard and stressful job. Our respect for them went up. They got to know us as well.

The second thing was unique as they began bringing us desserts. They were thanking us for helping them out. It was funny in a way. We were so into talking about sports that we were not aware that we were helping them. Our presence on the stage those days they were all running late was helping them. So they removed us from any extra duty schedules as we were extra crowd control in the cafeteria.

The third was learning about the students in our classes. We saw who they were running around with, what their behavior was during lunch, etc. We learned more about them. Seeing them outside of class explained a lot of things. It was educational.

After about 4 or 5 years we stopped eating in the cafeteria, due to the fact that my brother in law was throwing away 2 recliners, which I hauled up to school and put in my room. We moved the sports discussion to my room during lunch and laid back.

Maybe if we all understood each other better there would be less of a disconnect between the administration and the faculty in the average school. Seeing the world through the eyes of another person is a useful skill.

What would it be like to walk in their shoes? It seems like it is all too easy to stay in our own little world and forget that others live in a different and equally important one than we do. Trying to get along will go better the more we really understand the people at work.

So much to learn, right? Go for understanding in any and on all occasions. Who knows, you might wind up with an unexpected dessert. Yum.

Affirmation: I am a genius and I apply my wisdom.

38

FLIPPING THE CLASSROOM

I began hearing about the concept of the "flipped classroom" a few years ago. One of our principals was talking about how great it would be, as the students would watch the lecture at home and then do their assignments at school. This would solve the problem of our students not doing enough homework. After all, he said, research has proven this will work.

I was thinking, yeah, but research has proven a lot of other new utopian ideas in education would work, and when they were implemented at our school they did not work. Just how practical would the "flipped classroom" be?

I had my doubts if their idea would actually work, however, the intention was correct as we all know that our students do not do homework like we did when we were in high school. Getting the kids to actually do more work outside of class needed to happen, whatever it took.

It got me thinking about designing my own version of a flipped classroom. What would need to take place for the students to actually watch the lecture and take notes at home?

The first thing that needed to happen seemed to be a new name for the work at home, as I didn't want to call it a lecture. Hearing "lecture" might be enough for them to shut it down. I could imagine my students objecting: "I'm too busy, I'm not going to watch the lecture at home!", or "We don't have the INTERNET at my house, so there is no way I can watch the lecture at home!" They might also say they watched it when they didn't, or had 3 things playing at once and not actually be paying attention.

What would happen if I called watching the lecture a "take home video quiz?" How would they deal with that? All you have to do is take notes on these 10 videos, and when you turn it in, you will have a quiz grade of 100%! If it is late your maximum grade is a 70.

The following things happened when I began giving a take home video quiz:

1. Only half turned in their quiz on time the first couple of days. "You were serious?" they said. Yes. I eventually began getting almost all the take home video quizzes! They were not used to doing very much at all at home, so they were adjusting.

2. I got just a few contacts from parents about why their student had a zero on a take home video quiz. "You mean all they had to do was take notes on 10 problems? I'll see that they do this tonight!"

3. Some students said that at home, in their room, where it was all quiet with no distractions, they understood more of the material. Go figure.

4. It was easy to spot the ones who had just gone to the end of the video and copied the final solution. The next class day they didn't know what they were doing. I decided that it would be good idea to sometimes give a one question quiz at the beginning of class. I gave them one of the problems from the take home video quiz. It helped me know what the class understood.

5. I began to have thousands of views per month on my youtube clannel, lloyd4141. Go figure.

6. We had so many quiz grades that to avoid getting behind on data entry, I began entering the take

home video quiz grades before each period would leave my room. (2 to 3 minutes, I got faster, duh.)

7. The extra practice was paying off. They were getting the material faster than before.

8. I continued to assign homework as well as the take home video quiz. Take the video quiz which was the odd numbered problems, do the even ones for homework. They said that doing the even ones was much easier, since they were enough like the odd ones they had taken for the video quiz.

9. My tutorials in AP Statistics cut way down. Not as many students were lost. The even/odd routine was working very well for them.

10. This is the 7th school year I have been making and using videos. I have made about 3,950 videos of individual Algebra 2, PreCalculus and AP Statistics problems. Total views are about 700,000. I plan to continue to experiment with as many ways as possible to use videos to increase student learning and working outside of class. My Youtube sights are called lloyd41 and lloyd4141.

These days there are lots of sites where they can type in a problem and the computer will solve it for them. I prefer to make my own single problem videos.

No two of us math teachers explain things exactly the same way. So, my class flipping is only with me. My video making has become really fast as I work a problem as fast as possible. Since they have a pause button my speed is not a factor.

I also video my Test Keys because they have to do corrections outside of class for a daily grade. I attempt to keep all videos under a minute if possible. This way making videos for a 25 question Test can be done in about 30 minutes.

Any class can be flipped. Make your own videos. They can be used for years. You'll get fast. It's also interesting for me to watch my videos. It has changed my explanations some as I will think about things I wish I had said.

How much more work can you cause to happen outside of class? Give it a shot! Design it however it works for you. Drill vocabulary, short answers, important events, or have them make their own videos in whatever class you are teaching. No limits! Go! Go! Gadget!

Affirmation: I am a genius and I apply my wisdom.

39

DR. W'S SAGE ADVICE

Dr. W was our first assistant principal when we first opened the new high school. After the first year he was moved up to associate principal. His walk was similar to John Wayne's. Our faculty loved him.

When it was announced he was leaving we gave him a standing ovation in a faculty meeting. The superintendent was present and rushed to the mic and said, "If we could have only gotten Dr. W to accept one of our jobs, we wouldn't be losing him to another school district!"

I apologized to Dr. W for the superintendent lying. He grinned and said, "He threw salt on me didn't he!" I learned two very valuable lessons from Dr. W during his 3 years with us.

I was in his office one day talking about a student whose behavior was out of control. He got up and shut the door. He said what he was about to tell me was off the record, he would deny ever saying it, that it was messed up, but since it was just the way things were we all had to live with it. I had never heard the system of education so defined. It was an eye opening description.

He said that when I could not solve things on my level with an unruly student and it went to the assistant principal, that whatever the assistant principal decided to do I was not going to like, as I would disagree with the decision. He was right, I had already had that experience.

Then he said that when the assistant principal didn't solve things on their level, that it would get passed on up the chain to the associate principal, and whatever the associate principal did wasn't going to be pleasing to the assistant principal.

If the associate principal didn't solve it on their level it would go to the campus principal and whatever happened there was not going to be pleasing to the associate principal.

If the campus principal didn't solve the problem on their level then it would go over to the district office of the Deputy Superintendent of Secondary Schools, and then to the Superintendent and then to the school board.

Nobody likes the decision that gets made one level above them. Hmm. Lesson learned. I needed to learn to solve all problems on my level. Okay, I got it. There was no longer any need to complain about what any level above me was going to do. I might never agree with them anyway.

I began asking myself a different question when solving any problem with a student. "When the dust all settles and this problem is solved, what outcome am I willing to live with?"

We all make decisions at our level based on what stressors are involved. I learned to suit myself, negotiate the problem out with both the student and parents, and never let anything go a level above me, if at all possible!

What a change! How I would like things to turn out according to me when I have a problem with a student, is so much better than what happens if it ever leaves my hands.

I have solved all my own problems ever since. After all these years of problem solving it now seems obvious. Why did I ever expect those above me to settle things to my liking? They typically never did. Now they are out of the loop. They like it more because they never deal with any issue I have with a student or parent. I do.

Naturally, some issues have to go up stream, like truancy, physical violence, pot smoking, etc. All the other stuff belongs to me. So, how do you want things to turn out when it's all said and done? What outcome are you willing to live with?

Dr. W gave me another piece of good advice. It was in regards to how to deal with students that are emotionally disturbed.

They can cause disruptions, can't control some of their behaviors, and can dominate your class. He said to get them out in the hall and let them talk. They hardly ever feel like anybody listens to them. When do we give them a chance to get it off their chest and say whatever they want?

So what would you like to say? Then let them talk until they stop. Is that all? Would you like to add anything else? Let them talk some more. Are you sure you're done? Let them talk some more. I have been listening to you and when it is my turn to talk, you will not be allowed to interrupt me, so would you like to say anything else? Let them say whatever else they want. Ok, when I begin to talk you cannot interrupt, so are you sure you are through? They will finally be through.

Then I say, I have to control this entire class. When you are making lots of noise, I have to ask you to be quiet. When you feel a rush coming on, you have my permission to step outside my door for 1 minute and cool off. Can you make this work?

They almost always agree and are more controlled afterwards. All because I let them talk as much as they wanted. Just listening to them did the trick.

It does make me wonder what other problems I might be able to solve if I never interrupted anyone? I need to think about that one!

Affirmation: I am a genius and I apply my wisdom.

40

PROOFING TEACHING PROOFS

Several years ago one of my Geometry student's parents was what you might call a helicopter mom. She was doing everything she could to see that her son left high school fully prepared to succeed in college. She also volunteered at our school and was there almost every day.

Her son was a special education student whose disability was in oral expression. One of his modifications was that he would have an extra day to do all of his assignments. At his annual ARD meeting the question was asked if the extra day for assignments was necessary, given his disability in oral expression. Since all modifications have to be disability based I voted no. The assignments were not oral, so I did not see the need for the extra day.

This change to his modifications bothered his mom; she got a bee in her bonnet and was displeased with me. She felt like I had "led the charge" to have the extra day removed. She asked if it was okay if she visited my room during his class. Parents visiting class is high on my list, as I have an open door policy.

She came to class one day. As the kids were working she got up went to the book case and started thumbing through various students folders. I was not sure just what she was snooping around for, but decided not to confront her in front of a roomful of students about looking at other students work. She did not snoop long, took a seat at the back and was quiet and attentive.

When class was over she attacked me saying that the method I was using to teach proofs was wrong, not working and was not in the best interest of her son. Okay, I thought, that is the way she feels. I was wondering if her objection was in response to the events in the recent ARD. Maybe it was and maybe it wasn't.

I was having the students do each proof 5 times, in order to develop some frame of reference for the topic. The reason she said that it was not working and was not in the best interest of her son was because he had to write more and copying things was not good for him.

I tried to explain that after the 2nd time, I was pointing them toward doing the proof without looking, to see if they could follow the logical progression of steps, etc.

She shot back arguing that my method of teaching proofs was the most ridiculous thing she had ever seen.

I flipped the issue and said, "Well of all the things we teach in Geometry, proofs are among one of the hardest topics for us to teach and the students to grasp. For many of them it is their first experience into something so abstract. I have taught proofs about a dozen different ways over the years and have found that the five times routine works pretty well, but I am always open to new ideas. So how would you suggest I change the teaching of proofs so it would work better?"

Her jaw dropped. She was silent for a moment. She said she had no idea how to teach it but said that my method was not working. This ended our discussion. When the bell rang she left my room and was still upset.

I greeted her and said hello every time I saw her for the rest of the year. She moved her son to a different teacher the 2nd semester. My attempts to mend the fence and be helpful did not work.

All parents mean well. Sometimes it might be hard to see, when they come at us hard. I have tried harder since this experience with the proofs, to head off issues before they can even get started. I have been successful in doing so, most of the time.

Actually, it is better when a parent is involved to the extent that this mom was. She was doing her best to raise her son in the best way she knew how. I applaud her for her dedication to be an excellent parent. Just maybe she was right, too. Maybe I needed to find a better way to teach proofs.

I took a hard look at my process for teaching proofs. Logically speaking I had too many different kinds of proofs mixed together. The effect for the students was that most did not know how to do even one kind at the end of the unit. Okay, feedback accepted, so what did I need to do about it?

I arranged the proofs into categories and we practiced one category at a time. The first category I picked was given the name 180 degree proofs. They all included either 2 triangles, 2 lines, or one triangle and one line. The sum of the angles of a triangle equal 180 degrees. Every line has 180 degrees. I had the students practice the 180 degree proofs until they could do them in their sleep.

I noticed as I added the other categories that they were getting them faster, because some of the various parts of the 180 degree proofs were used again.

The lesson I learned again was: chunk the material at a gradient where it is impossible to not succeed.

I am thankful for this mom as she made me question my methods. She helped make me a better teacher.

The other thing I learned from this experience was that there is no such thing as criticism. It is all feedback. What does the feedback we get say about our jobs as teachers? Lashing out at the feedback doesn't help in the long run, because we did not take the feedback and adjust our processes.

Whereas it is true that our parents might know nothing about teaching math, they know a ton about their own kids. We need to accept their feedback, instead of dismissing them as people who know nothing about teaching. Questioning our methods is always a good thing. I question mine every day. How else would I be able to grow?

Feedback is your friend. Embracing it will make it possible for you to change, adjust and grow.

Affirmation: I am a genius and I apply my wisdom.

41

INSTANT FEEDBACK

After a department meeting one year at my former school, I found myself thinking a lot about Mr. Simonds comments about the kids never getting any feedback between the review and the Test. His thought was that if they were not clear when doing the review because they have something off a little bit, how would they know to correct it before they took the Test? How will we know to correct them, too? He made an excellent point. The question then became: How can I assess their mastery of the review? What do I need to do about their gaps in knowledge, if any exist?

I began to make all my reviews, video reviews. Then following the 5 times routine, I would award 10 points on the Test if the review is done 5 times. It was amazing how many kids actually did the review 5 times. I have them staple it to their Test before they turn it in and do not let them use it while taking their Test.

I discovered that making a play list of 25 videos for the average Test was easy. I would go to the 5 or 6 pages of problems the Test was covering, see how many videos I already had made from those pages, select 4 or 5 from each page, click them and create a new play list. I would pseudo match the Test questions with like problems. With the videos already made, creating the playlist was a 10-minute task. I began to post the video review a week or two before each Test. Playlist creation on YouTube is extremely easy, you will like it.

Final exam reviews were just longer. This past term the Pre-AP Algebra 2 Final Review had 77 videos and the on level Algebra 2 had 54 videos. I had the Final Video Reviews posted a month before the final. The Spring Finals this year covered about 400 pages from our textbook, so I made sure they had the review as early as possible.

I have actually had kids make an A on the final that were in danger of failing, as they finally became organized. Sometimes they have turned in a review that was very thick. The repetition of each problem done correctly wound up helping them master any concept with which they had an issue.

The other positive change for me was review days in class. I used to dread them as getting the kids to work was difficult at times. Once the video reviews began, they would be on their smart device or laptop with ear buds and the room would be very quiet. I might get as many as six or seven questions during a 50-minute class.

One day during a review, my door opened and the Associate Principal walked in with 4 other adults to observe my class. I was not sure just what they would think about the kids all being on smart devices, but they loved it.

Get your video making going, watch any of mine you like on YouTube at lloyd41, or lloyd4141, and the more you play around with making videos, just how you choose to use videos, the more you are going to like it. Having fun at work is always a great thing. Go for it.

Affirmation: I am a genius and I apply my wisdom.

42

THE FIST FIGHT IN ALGEBRA

Once upon a time, things were going pretty well in Algebra class. I had the students working in groups. All of a sudden, 2 guys across the room from where I was helping a group, jumped up and started trading punches to the face.

They had hit each other 3 or 4 times before I could get over there to break it up. I got them out in the hall and told them they were going to the office and their parents would be called and they would be suspended.

They immediately apologized; started shaking hands and tried to convince me to not take them to the office. I told them that as soon as the bell rang to dismiss class the news would spread all over school. The fight story would spread like wildfire. Sure enough, the bell rang and my other students were talking about it as they left the room.

I took the boys down to the office and they were sent home and suspended for the next day.

A few hours passed and our Assistant Principal came to get me. One of the boys' moms worked at the school next door. She came over after school and was insisting her son not be suspended as the other kid had started it.

The Assistant Principal tried to explain to her that he was suspended. She argued back that he would get behind on his Algebra studies and that he had to be in class the next day. Do I have to go to the Superintendent's office, she threatened?

They kept arguing for another 10 minutes, neither one willing to budge. I wanted to stop the argument. Just how could I do that? What could I say that would end the discussion?

I told the mom that I did not want her son in class the next day. It would send the wrong message to all my other students and I did not want them thinking they could exchange blows during class because there would not be any consequences. I told her I would make sure her son did not get behind.

She said ok and left. As a classroom teacher she got it. I wanted to control my class. Open season on fist fighting in Algebra was not something I could let occur. Her son needed to face the consequences. The Assistant Principal thanked me later for helping him out of a jam.

I did not have any more issues with those 2 boys for the rest of the year. Being consistent when assigning consequences for unruly behavior might be hard to do, especially when the parents want something different. Even when it is hard, apply the consequences as consistently as possible. Tell all parents what you need to happen in order to manage your class effectively. They will appreciate where you are coming from, even if they do not agree.

Come to think of it, another one of my Principals made up a new word one day over the intercom. He said if there were any senior pranks pulled that year that you would all be *consequenced*! His new word made me smile. That's funny right there.

Affirmation: I am a genius and I apply my wisdom.

43

VIDEO MAKING

A former student called me one June day asking if she could come to my house for some tutoring on a Test the local community college was having her take. I didn't want to do it, but didn't know how to tell her no. When she asked me what I would charge I said $100, thinking that would scare her away. She said that would be great and came over for 2 hours.

After she left my wife asked me what was wrong. I said I was worn out and would not be doing any more tutoring from the house during the summer. Then I had the thought that If I had a bunch of problems worked on video that I could tutor anybody without having to even show up.

I called a colleague and we set a day to meet up at school so I could learn how to make videos and upload them onto YouTube. My first YouTube channel was born.

The next fall I began to make videos during the school year. By the first of December I had made about 300 Pre-Cal videos. The videos were from 1 to 5 minutes long, as each one was of a single problem. A few of them were closer to 10 minutes, due to the difficulty of the problem, like harmonic motion word problems.

Some of the students had been watching some of them. I discovered that almost all the A students were watching them multiple times. Some of the students that needed the extra work were not using the extra help. Hmm. What to do about that?

A thought did not occur to me until our Pre-Cal team was planning the final exam. Let's make the final exam review all video. If you turn in the review you get a small bonus on the final exam. We picked out about 50 problems for the final video review.

We gave the students the video review 2 weeks before the final. It was hyper linked, so they could just click on the number of the problem and the video would play. There were 5,000 views in 10 days. All the students who actually did the video review made 80 or higher on the final. Every Test during the spring semester had a video review. The views continued to grow as we would find new ways to get them to work outside of class time.

The second year I kept making videos for both AP Stats and Pre-Cal. I got up to about 800 made. Year 3 has grown to about 1,400 videos and 107,000 views. I keep finding ways to use these videos. Will it ever stop? Today it is 3,925 videos made and 700,138 views.

Seven years have passed since I began making videos. I also have changed schools and no longer teach AP Stats or Pre-Calculus. I have become the Algebra 2 department at a private school. This year I am making Algebra 2 videos. I have already made 1620 videos of individual problems. My students have watched them 244,266 times. I have 75 students compared to around 160 from prior years.

I am giving more take home video quizzes, because I want my students to take notes at home. If I ever run out of time in class, I just have them learn from the videos at home. The videos are all odd numbered problems and the balance of each assignment are even problems.

My main purpose for making videos is to help my students work outside of class. Not every student uses them, but they are available at all times via YouTube. If they are absent for any reason, they can use the video instruction to catch up. All test reviews are 100% video. I want them to take notes and practice by doing each review problem 5 times. If they do they get a small bonus on their test. When they actually do the review for learning, they always make an 80 or higher on the test.

Just how many ways could you get your students to work outside of class? I'm not sure, but getting them to work more outside of class will only help them. Use videos if you want, or not. It's up to you. If you decide to start making videos of various math problems you will find yourself watching them all, just to see what they look like and to observe yourself teaching. I have grown and changed a lot just by watching myself. If you are teaching Pre-Calculus, AP Stats or Algebra 2, use my videos if you like on YouTube at lloyd4141 (AP Stats and Pre-Cal) or lloyd41 (Algebra 2).

Make them work more and college will be easier for them. Duh.

Affirmation: I am a genius and I apply my wisdom.

44

UTILIZING T-SHIRTS

Utilization means to use all events that occur to the benefit of achieving your goal. If something happens in class, utilize it to make a point pointing towards your goal. I used to brush events off or just ignore them. Now I utilize them to help what I'm trying to get done.

Once upon time when I was speaking at church, I made a somewhat humorous comment that got some laughter. A couple of minutes later someone laughed very loud. They were just slow getting it. Since the audience heard it, which was a distraction, I paused and said something to the effect that some jokes that are told on Wednesday get a laugh on Sunday. This comment tied a bow around the distraction, so to speak. It was also a great break state. Use any and all events to advantage.

I never intended to utilize t-shirts in any way in any of my classes. I had actually never even thought about it. Generally, I attempt to avoid anything that involves fundraisers or handling money at school. It's one less thing to deal with.

The first t-shirt scenario happened as a tag on to the *FREAKONOMICS* Reading. One of my very good longtime friends gave me the book *FREAKONOMICS* the summer before I began teaching Advanced Placement Statistics. *FREAKONOMICS* has a unique spin on what real Statistics actually are. It is a great read and highly recommended.

How could I utilize this book to advantage in the AP Stats classes? Hmm..... What would happen, I wondered, if we had a *FREAKONOMICS* Reading one day during class? How would I want to do it and when would be the best time? I picked the Friday before Spring break. They often are restless that day as they are anticipating their holiday. I added the *FREAKONOMICS* Reading to my schedule.

I would need a class set of the *FREAKONOMICS* book. Our Associate Principal took care of that for me. The books came in and were stashed in the library.

I decided to have one big reading group. We would just go around the room, up and down each row of students, each reading a paragraph. How would my students react? Would they just think that it was dumb like the reading groups in elementary school? They did, until the story we were reading grabbed them.

We read Chapter 3 in *FREAKONOMICS: WHY DRUG DEALERS STILL LIVE WITH THEIR MOMS?* It is a very interesting story and has some intense moments. The authors didn't edit out the bad language and various racial slurs. I instructed the class to skip the obscene language. It wound up being humorous, as the reader tended to pause on those words.

The reading was a big success. My friend and his wife came and participated in the reading. So did one of the librarians. They read when it was their turn and had a great time. Just before they left my friends wife said we needed to make a T-Shirt. It could say *THERE'S A STAT FOR THAT* on the front and *FREAKONOMICS CHAPTER 3: WHY DRUG DEALERS STILL LIVE WITH THEIR MOMS?* on the back. She suggested a black shirt with white lettering.

This idea came out of the blue. I didn't want to do it. Seemed like too much trouble. So I sucked it up and ordered the shirts. Why not utilize the opportunity to build some momentum from the reading? We bought the shirts the first year. The shirts were sold at cost in the following years. When the shirts came in the students who ordered one were excited and chose a day to wear them to school. It created a buzz on our campus. No other class had a class t-shirt. All righty then!

The craziest thing that happened was 20 extra students signed up to take AP Statistics the following year. I received some kudos for doing such a great recruiting job. How did you do it Massie? I said it's crazy, make a t-shirt, get 20 additional students.

I've also been asked what's it's all about when I wear the shirt in public. Just, *"Why Do Drug Dealers Still Live with Their Moms?"* they ask. I tell them, *There's A Stat For That!* The reason is they are only making about $3 an hour selling drugs, hoping for a chance to move up eventually, so they have to live with their moms. The *FREAKONOMICS* Reading was repeated all 6 years I taught AP Statistics. When I left and became the Algebra 2 Department at a private school the reading ceased.

T-Shirt number 2 occurred at my new school, because my students began asking why we didn't have an official Algebra 2 T-Shirt? At the time, I thought it wasn't a bad idea, but since I had never designed a t-shirt, I thought that it wasn't going to happen. The idea took life. Current and former students wanted an Algebra 2 T-Shirt. All righty then, so I said I would think about it.

A former student heard about it and asked if she could design our Algebra 2 T-Shirt. I told her to go for it. "Just what are you thinking about", I asked. She said she was thinking about using some Massie-isms.

There are Massie-isms? The truth hurts. I apparently say them often. OK. My various Massie-isms are for the most part sarcastic. They include:

1. *Yippy Skippy.*
2. *See you around like a donut.*
3. *Give me strength.*

4. *Dream On.*
5. *Thank you for that mind boggling trivia.*
6. *I'll alert the media.*
7. *Shut up and have a good time.*
8. *I'm so excited.*
9. *"This is your conscience; I really want to pass this class." (I whisper this one.)*
10. *I hate it when my girlfriend calls me during class. What will my wife say? (They know my girlfriend is also my wife.)*
11. *All righty then.*

She used 2 Massie-isms from the list and created a colorful Algebra 2 T-shirt. *YIPPY SKIPPY Algebra 2* is on the front and the back has a pile of donuts and the phrase *SEE YOU AROUND LIKE A DONUT.* When I asked the principal for his approval he said he had already heard about it and thought it was a great idea. He suggested that we put HP somewhere on the shirt for Hyde Park, the name of our school. So an HP was added.

The *Yippy Skippy* T-Shirt was born. They were sold at cost. All orders were handled on line and a bunch sold. I gave one to the entire math department, too. We occasionally have a *Yippy Skippy* day. The word will spread around school and we'll all wear them on some designated Friday. On *Yippy Skippy* day lots of group photos are always taken. Now many of my incoming students ask when the t-shirts will be available.

I initially thought this was going to be too much trouble. It wasn't. It has had the effect of making things more interesting and fun. Fun is good. So just what else would my students get excited about that would help liven things up? Good question.

"This is your conscience; utilize any and all events to build interest and push towards your goal. *Yippy Skippy! See You Around Like A Donut.*"

Affirmation: I am a genius and I apply my wisdom.

45

PRESSURED TO CHANGE A GRADE

Once upon a time, I was pressured to change a grade. The starting offensive tackle had failed the first trimester of Geometry for the third consecutive time. He needed to make a 37 on the final exam to pass. He made a 17. Our football team was in the playoffs.

The head football coach called me and asked what kind of extra credit his player could do to pass. He said that he had to have him the next week, providing we won the game on Saturday. I said my policy was to give extra credit assignments that anyone could do and that I did not give an extra credit assignment just so someone could pass. I had already turned in my grades. The first trimester was over. I was not willing to doctor the grade.

He said he did not want the grade doctored, but that an extra credit assignment should pull him up to passing. I said no. He said that if we won Saturday that he and Mr. B, our campus principal, would have a meeting with me on Monday.

I suppose that the rationalization is that the extra credit will cover over the changing of a grade. Maybe the extra pressure from Mr. B. would get me to give in and I would just change it. If I refused, there would have been some kind of repercussion. My schedule might change. I could get a bad evaluation. Would they renew my contract? They would have done something in retaliation, under the guise of something else.

We lost the game on Saturday. The coach never called me again. I was glad. I lost all respect for the coach. It must be much easier to just pressure and bully faculty members than getting his players to pass on their own. I suspected this coach had pressured many teachers over the course of his career.

I have often wondered what I would have done to protect myself, if the meeting with the coach and principal had actually happened. The only thought I had at the time was to call the local sports writer and have him sit in on the meeting. Today I would most likely call my association representative to sit in, or call the University Interscholastic League and seek their advice.

About 18 years after the coach had called pressuring me for an extra credit assignment, I was listening to a sports radio call in show on the way home one night, and the topic was about how a school in Texas had lost the state title in football, because they had played an ineligible player on 2 kickoffs. The host had a retired coach on the air as his expert on integrity in coaching. I did not hear the beginning of the show.

After the commercial break the host introduced the coach. It was same guy that had pressured me. I got home, called in, got on the air, and hung up. I decided that if I were the host, the last thing that I would want would be my expert on integrity to be exposed as a fraud on the air.

I sent him an email instead, a few days later. The host responded quickly, thanked me for the heads up and for helping him to avoid the embarrassment. It was better that way, as a coach with no integrity would have just lied and said he had never pressured anyone to change a grade, not him. Trust and integrity can be fragile. They can take a long time to build and can be lost in a flash.

My suggestion for you is to think about this scenario in advance, just in case you find yourself in the same situation one day. Come up with a plan of how you will handle it. I had never thought about it before and was blindsided when the coach called to pressure me.

My new plan is to inform the coach that I am calling the interscholastic league to report grade irregularities and pressure to change a failing grade to passing. My association representative will also be attending any meeting where I will be pressured to change a grade under the guise of an extra credit assignment.

While we are thinking about it, how many other scenarios of various kinds, should we all be getting ready for that might occur in our future? What will our plan be if blindsided? How will we handle it? What will be our desired outcome be? Hmm.

Affirmation: I am a genius and I apply my wisdom.

46

STATISTICALLY INSIGNIFICANT

Statistically insignificant are words we often use when teaching Statistics. It means that there would be no change or a change so small in our statistic that we would just ignore it, as it would not mean anything.

Therefore, when we compare test scores for this year's sophomores with last year's sophomores, for example, if the change is 1 point or less, we would say it's *statistically insignificant*. A change that small could be explained by the fact that we tested 700 different people than we tested last year.

One day this year in Pre-AP Algebra 2 my students had already worked about 25 problems in class and I felt like they had the concept down, so I was thinking about not assigning homework, when they began begging me not to assign homework. I was not going to let them think that they could ever talk me out of an assignment, so I said, "Who would like an assignment that would add 5 points to their lowest test grade!" They switched and all wanted to do the assignment. I gave them a video play list with 25 videos on it as the assignment. All they had to do was take notes from the videos. The next day they had all done the assignment.

They were clueless as to what the effect of having a test grade raised 5 points would actually do to their average. The most that it changed an average was 1 point. The students with high averages only changed from something like 98.2 to 98.3. All the changes were actually *statistically insignificant*.

I had found another way to get them to watch a 40-minute lecture from home and like it. To watch the 25 videos and take notes on them took about 40 minutes. No one noticed the fact that the impact on his or her grade was *statistically insignificant*. Check it out and you will see I'm right. The overall average won't hardly change at all.

We grade on 9-week grading periods. I might have 4 to 5 tests per quarter. If your school is on 6-week grading periods and you only give 2 tests during that time, the most the test average could move would be 2.5 points, still really small. Throw in daily grades and quizzes and the overall average might not even move that much.

The other factor in their rush to watch a 40 minute lecture is the fact that their grades mean more to them than they do to us. They might do any assignment you give if they believe it will make their average rise.

I'm thinking that I won't use this technique very often as I don't want to let the cat out of the bag, but it just might work best toward the end of a grading period, as the very thought that their average could go up would be enough to get them going.

Hmm, how many other ways could we give an assignment and have our students all excited about getting it done? Good question! I wish I knew all the other ways, too.

Affirmation: I am a genius and I apply my wisdom.

47

THE DAY I WAS A TOTAL ABYSMAL FAILURE

One day I went into the office of my appraiser for my end of the year conference. The formal evaluation was already done. The summative as they call it, was most often a formality. We would usually discuss items on the formal evaluation and school procedural items involving following school policies.

My appraiser had a long computer printout spread out on her desk. She began by saying that she had been looking at my Geometry student's grades for grading period 5 and that they were good. Then she mentioned that my Geometry grades for grading period 4 had been very bad.

Then she said, "Mr. Massie, I would like to know what you did to be such a big success in Geometry during grading period 5, since we both know you were a *total abysmal failure* during grading period 4?"

Well, that was not what I was expecting. I decided to blow her mind. Blowing her mind would be easy, I was thinking, for a single reason. It is impossible to be able to tell what is going on in any class just by looking at a computer printout. There are just too many lurking variables, which could explain the grades on the printout.

I have known many administrators that have attempted to analyze the success of a teacher based on the grades on the page. It is extremely difficult to get a correct assessment, just from the print out.

Another year, my supervisor had talked to me about my grading period grades, saying that they all looked good, but in one class my failure rate was 18% and I needed to get it under 10%. Why was it so high, he asked? I replied, that the class in question only had 16 students and the 3 that had failed had each been absent 8 times or more and had lots of missing assignments. Oh, he said, then you're ok!

There is always a reason why grades can be low one grading period and take a jump the next one. I will admit that one of the possible reasons is that I might have been a *total abysmal failure*. It was not the case this time. Over reacting to her calling me a *total abysmal failure* wasn't going to get me anywhere, so I stayed calm.

I said, "Well, I knew that was going to happen!"

She asked, "Then why didn't you do something to prevent it?"

I said, "Well, I have been trying the last several years to prevent the grades from taking a big drop during grading period 4, and have tried a bunch of different methods to keep it from happening, but have not, as yet, found the solution."

She said, "So what's the problem?"

I said, "Every year we are cruising along in Geometry and our grades are all in the upper ranges and then we get to grading period 4 and they take a dive, because, we finally get to the hardest material in the book! We get through it and the grades in grading period 5 go back to the normal level."

Her jaw dropped. The lurking variable was we were studying the hardest material in the book. Some material is harder than other material! Duh. The grades always dropped in grading period 4.

She said, "So that's why all the Geometry grades in the whole school took a dive during grading period 4!"

She did not apologize for calling me a *total abysmal failure*.

I said, "Actually it seems to be worse this year, because we don't have the student tutors in class anymore!"

She said, "Student tutors, I didn't know we had any student tutors? Who are they and where did they go?"

I said, "We have been using our freshman in Geometry as tutors for years."

She said," Wait, wait, wait, that makes no sense. How can a freshman be tutoring a sophomore?"

I said, "The freshman took Algebra 1 as 8th graders. They are on the track that leads to Calculus their senior year. They almost always make "A's" in Geometry. We ask them to help us tutor anybody that is struggling. When our 9th grade center opened this year, we lost them to the school next door. We also lost their high grades and Test scores, so our overall Geometry grades are lower than prior years."

She said, "That's why our grades in Geometry are down across the board this year. I have been trying to figure this out. Thanks, I got it."

I wanted to ask her if she was going to take back the *total abysmal failure* comment, but I didn't. She didn't apologize for it either. I wasn't surprised. At least I was only a *total abysmal failure* for less than 1 minute. Lol.

The real *total abysmal failure*, however, is anytime any of us make a decision without first asking the resident expert, whoever the resident expert might be. Maybe the resident expert closest to you resides in the math department, maybe they don't.

And just a suggestion, it might be a good idea to consider any and all lurking variables that could be controlling the outcome you see in any grade book, before rushing to a judgment that is incorrect. Hmm... those lurking variables, I wonder just how many there might be?

Affirmation: I am a genius and I apply my wisdom.

48

THREATENED IF I DIDN'T
PART 1

I wish that I could tell you that you would never be thrown under the bus at the school where you are working. Unfortunately, a lot of backstabbing tends to happen. Of course, you could be lucky and never be backstabbed, or not.

I have been wondering just how to advise you regarding all the interpersonal relationships you will have at any school where you ever happen to work. The best place to begin is in your subject department, then branch out to all other groups in your building.

One idea I heard years and years ago has served me well. It is to build as strong a relationship as possible with all the administrative assistants in the building. So make friends with the librarian, assistant librarian, receptionist, secretaries, counselors, janitors, etc. The principals' administrative assistant at times knows more about what is going on in a school than the principal does. I build as many bridges as I can.

Be yourself and be nice to them. There are too many horror stories about how some faculty members treat all the administrative assistants. Sometimes they have been treated with total contempt. Doing the opposite and treating them like you want to be treated is the thing to do. If the women that work in the office begin to place all their own children in your classes, it is a great sign you have built strong relationships.

I was a little slow figuring this one out. Eventually, I

knew it was not a mistake that I kept getting the kids of the librarians, two registrars, various counselors, assistant principals, teachers, etc. If an occasion arose where I needed some help from anyone in the office, people were ready and willing to help me. For example, I got a call one day during first period informing me my sister's battle with ALS had ended. I went straight to the Associate Principal's administrative assistant's office. I told her I needed to leave school, she said go, I will take care of things. She did.

She also helped me with parking permits, faxes, employee paperwork, as well as a host of other things over the 17 years I worked there. Each time I would see her she would catch me up on how her two boys were doing in college, as I had taught them Pre-Calculus. She left our school a few years ago. I saw her at a church we were visiting a while back. She was excited to see me and we had a good chat.

Build strong relationships. Treat everyone the same way you do your favorite aunt or uncle.

Okay, you are right again; I began talking about being thrown under the bus and stalled saying anything about it. So, keep reading because that is what is coming next.

Affirmation: I am a genius and I apply my wisdom.

49

THREATENED IF I DIDN'T
PART 2

I hope a colleague never stabs you in the back. However, it has happened to me many times. Think through just what you will do if it ever happens to you. Rose-colored glasses regarding backstabbing might turn out to be a mistake.

Here is one example that happened to me. I was asked to teach Advance Placement Statistics and promised that if I would the rest of my schedule would be 4 Pre-Calculus classes. On the last day of school, I was informed that I would not be teaching Pre-Calculus the next year but would have 4 classes of Math Modeling instead.

I asked why. The answer was that a teacher we had hired would not be able to handle the unruly behaviors in Math Modeling, so he would be teaching Pre-Calculus. I asked why we were hiring someone who we knew could not handle our students. I was told that I could talk to the Associate Principal but that nothing could be done.

The real reason for this particular schedule change was that our department chair worked for an alternative certification program on the side and was trying to protect one of her alternative certification people from having a bad schedule. Give me strength.

The next year I would lose my favorite class to teach and have two classes that I had never taught. I would also never trust our department chair again. Sounds like an opportunity to grow, right?

Therefore, what choices do we all have when we feel violated like this and trust has been lost? Here are some ideas:

1. Cool down. Wait until you cool off for 3 days before you do anything. This is the thing to do. As it turned out, after 2 months had past it became known that our department chair had created a big mess with several teachers in our department. My schedule was then changed to 2 AP Stats, 3 Pre-Calculus and 1 math modeling class. I was asked a few times when school started back if I was okay, as the word was out that I had been given a raw deal. The truth is impossible to hide. So stay calm. Things can eventually work themselves out by just biding your time.

2. Consider the fact that God is changing your schedule for some good reasons. Being forced, as it were, to learn to teach AP Stats, which was very difficult the first 2 years, is the best thing that happened to me during the 17 years I taught at that high school. The AP Stats program grew to 4 sections, kids were standing in line to take it the next year, I was the only one teaching it so nobody was trying to steal it from me. I'm on a first name basis with the Department Chair of Statistics at Texas A & M. Teaching AP Stats turned out to be a lot of fun. Come to think of it, I always pray that God will do whatever is really best for me regardless of what it is. The best thing for me was to learn to teach AP Stats.

3. Become guarded. I was extremely careful whom I trusted after this particular backstabbing. I was much quieter afterwards and would only discuss any happenings at school with Kevin or Tricia. I knew that I could trust them.

4. Keep your mouth shut. Everything you say can potentially get back to the person you say it about. Practice the golden rule even if you are the only one that does so in your building. "Do unto others as you would have them do unto you!" This is a quote of course from Jesus Christ, the Son

of God.

Looking back I know that God used the teaching of AP Stats to build me up around our school in ways that I could have never even dreamed myself. I would have also missed getting to teach Miss Griffith, who is the most brilliant person that ever walked into my classroom.

Affirmation: I am a genius and I apply my wisdom.

50

THREATENED IF I DIDN'T
Part 3
TIME TO FORGIVE

Now, a word about forgiving.

My baby sister died of ALS in October of 2015 at the age of 60. Her 3-year struggle was fought with grace and dignity. When she was first diagnosed, our entire family was shaken, of course, and I began searching for anyone who had ever been healed of ALS. I found a man who had co-authored a book about healing whose story was how he was healed of his ALS. I ordered the book and read it while we were on Thanksgiving break. One of the tasks he assigned was forgiveness. I was to make a list of everyone who had ever harmed me in my life and go about forgiving them all.

I went back to my earliest memories and would write down a name, pray for them and let it go. All the way through the history of my life the journey went, as I kept asking, who have I not forgiven yet? Teachers, friends, family, people at school, church, guys on sports teams, professors, Dr. Green, bosses, principals, colleagues, and on and on I journeyed, including the 2 ladies who had thrown me under the bus, when my schedule was shafted.

WOW!!!

What a relief! It felt great to forgive. At the same time I was wondering, what it would be like when I bumped into either one of those women again? Sure enough, one of them was in my group a year later in a staff training. We talked and interacted in our group. My emotions were flat. That feedback said that I had actually forgiven her and let it go. As far as my side of the fence was concerned, I had done what

I could to settle things.

A month or so later the visiting speaker at our church was a guy from my college days. He praised my sister and then poured salt on me, trying to tell a little joke. He was the only one who laughed. My emotions flared up a bit. It hit me that I had not forgiven him, yet. So, I got busy during his lesson forgiving him. After the service, I bought his book in the lobby, and he repeated the same salt pouring comment. My emotions were flat. Ok, one more person forgiven.

A few months later, I remembered that I had not forgiven a thug at my school growing up who had bullied me. So, ok get busy forgiving him. I saw him last month at a college reunion. My emotions were flat again. I went up and talked to him for a while. We had a good conversation.

It does not matter who I like, trust, or who I want to hang around, all that really matters is if I forgive. The bullying happened when I was in the 7th & 8th grade. It left some scars. I can still feel the scars, but no longer have any negative emotions towards him. Unbelievably, he has made an eternal impact on many hundreds of orphans, as he has been the man in charge of a children's home for over 30 years. This has been his life's work. His dad died when he was young. He and his brothers were thugs in his early days. He changed. Thankfully, we have all changed since Junior High.

"Forgive us our trespasses as we forgive those who trespass against us! Deliver us from evil!"

Holding grudges will only hurt you. Forgiving will bring peace. Settle all old wounds with any person who ever hurt you and forgive them. You will most likely never ever see them again. It is time for you to be free and let it go.

As the wise man said, "As much as in you is, be at peace with all men."

Affirmation: I am a genius and I apply my wisdom.

51

RIOT IN THE CAFETERIA

Back when the state of Texas was giving the TAAS Test, our school made the decision that on the 3 TAAS Test days, since the seniors would not be at school, we could get by with 2 lunches instead of 3. It sounded like a good idea. It turned out to be a disaster.

Mr. Christensen and I were sitting at the faculty table in the corner of the cafeteria eating our lunch. We were talking about sports, like we always did at lunch, when the shouting started. There was one group of about 75 students on the stage shouting and cussing at another group of 75 students on the other side of cafeteria.

A guy came from each group towards the middle of the cafeteria, took off their t-shirts and started fighting. The policeman and a principal separated them and escorted them to the office. The shouting continued.

I said, "Oh no! We are the only adults left in here!"

Mr. Christensen and I walked to the center of the cafeteria and stood back to back, as the 2 groups rushed towards each other. It was pretty scary. We managed to keep them at bay until the principal came back. She moved one group outside the cafeteria in the hallway, but they stopped just outside the door and continued shouting and cussing at the other group. The group inside rushed the doors. We managed to keep them in the cafeteria, but just barely. It was one interesting lunch.

The problem started when 750 students were sent to the cafeteria that only had 600 chairs. It continued when the

169

cafeteria ran out of food. It escalated when one girl called another one the B word. Things got out of control really fast.

The next 2 days the same schedule was repeated. Mr. Christensen and I ate lunch off campus. The next 2 years they kept the same schedule, 2 lunches instead of the normal 3, on TAAS Test days.

There was an unwillingness to change plans. Changing the plan would have been an admission that the plan had failed. So the attempt was made to try harder to make a plan that was destined to fail work. It never did.

Our pride can sure get in the way of logic. All of us in education have kept doing things that have already been proven not to work. Everyone already knows that a change needs to be made. So changing from a plan destined to fail to any other plan is always better. If the 2nd plan doesn't work either, try plan 3.

And just maybe it's a good idea to do a little math. 600 - 750 = -150 Do you really want to send 750 people somewhere when there are only 600 chairs? Not me. Looks like a math problem.

Affirmation: I am a genius and I apply my wisdom.

52

THE LINE AND THE PAGE PRINTER

One day during my senior year in high school, May 1970, I went with my girlfriend to drop off some paperwork to her brother- in-law. He was the data base manager at a Farah slacks factory. The computers were about twice as big as a side by side refrigerator. There were at least 6 of them. Johnny was feeding stacks of cards through the computer and printing reports.

While they were talking, I wondered over to a printer that was using the very wide computer paper. The paper was coming up out of a box on the floor and passing under this bar, where the report was printed and then refolding in a big stack on the floor on the other side. Johnny saw me staring at the printing and asked what I thought about it.

I had never seen anything like that, wasn't sure what it was, or what was happening and generally was clueless about computers. Johnny said I was watching a line printer. It was printing a whole line with a single stroke, which made it seem like the paper was flying.

"Wow", I said, "That's really fast." "No", Johnny said, "The computer is many thousands of times faster than the printer. Come back next week and you'll get to see the new page printer." "Page printer? ", I said, "Yeah", Johnny said, "It will print a whole page with one stroke." "Wow", I said, "Then that will really be fast!" "No", Johnny said," the computer is still many thousands of times faster." Keep this story in mind.

I made a mistake and never went back to see the page

printer. They had one though, to use with those massive first generation computers. Today our laser printers or even single character printers do a much better job, while using regular paper and the computer is still many thousands of times faster.

In 1997 I joined Round Rock ISD as a math teacher at Round Rock High School. I had 3 classes of Algebra 1 Extended, as they called the class in those days. The students were all historically low performers as they had failed Algebra 1 the year before, had not had any success to speak of, in any math class and had been placed into a double block class. On a normal block schedule classes meet every other day. These classes met every day, meaning that I had twice as much time to teach these kids.

The performance of the students was generally low. They were making tons of what they called, when I was in school, "mental mistakes". These included, but are not limited to, miscopying, poor penmanship, mistakes with arithmetic, sign rules violations, exponent law goof ups, as well as many other mistakes that could be clumped in a group called "mental mistakes".

I went in search of a way to cut out all "mental mistakes". First, I determined not to use the term "mental mistake". There is too much negative baggage with the term. I never liked being told that I was "mental", and figured that this was the last thing that anyone else would want to hear. I would also need a new catch phrase to replace "mental mistake". I came up with "*la boo boo*", said in the best Pepe La Pew voice I could muster. (For you youngsters, Pepe La Pew was a skunk. He became a famous cartoon character popular for his french accent and peculiar odor).

I began to wonder why it has always been common for students learning Algebra to make these kinds of errors. How is it possible that students from all generations, while learning Algebra, historically have made these kinds of "*la boo boos*"?

I thought back to my experience in the computer room at Farah Slacks in 1970. I had an idea. Just maybe the explanation for all the "*la boo boos*" was the simple fact that our computer was going many thousands of times faster than our printer, which was usually a no. 2 pencil. Was it possible that the speed at which the brain was working, meant that it was always way far ahead of the speed of our pencils, and the mistakes were the result? How could I make them slow down their brains?

Slowing down their brains turned out to be very easy to do. Of course the contradiction is obvious, right? I was about to take students who had been habitually low performers and slow down their brains. Crazy idea, isn't it? The idea got a big laugh from the math department, as well.

While this was being tested, to see if the fact our pencil can't keep up was really the issue, I also needed to make them organize their work in a way where they could both read it correctly and not skip anything. They balked at using more room, writing bigger, as well as not being sold on the slow down my brain process they were being asked to adopt.

We had plenty of time. So the experiment began.

To make them slow their brain down, I told them that from now on I expected their work to be done in 4 colors. I handed out four colors of bic pens to each student. And we began to practice. The "*la boo boos*" immediately dropped by 50%. Within a week they were down 85%.

Sun Hee was a girl from Viet Nam who could not speak much English. She had failed Algebra 1 the year before. She began using four colors of ink and her work started looking like an art project. It had zero mistakes and was beautiful. She made A+ for the rest of the year. I would grade my answer key with her paper. From her I learned to have the students make all negative signs in red, positives signs in green, variables in black and exponents in blue.

In the micro seconds between laying down one pen and picking up another one, we had slowed down the brain just enough to allow the printer to keep up. The brain now had an additional task of color coding, so it stopped racing towards the end of the problem.

My message became: I want you to slow down your computer (brain), so your printer (pencil) can keep up. Of course, I tell the story about the line and page printer. The students relate to this story. It helps them to take their time.

And in one of the greatest serendipities of the whole process, as strange as it may seem, they were doing their work faster. They had adopted a new and improved process of writing down their work, they were using a lot more space to work in, as well as a lot more paper and four colors of ink, their mistakes were at a bare minimum and they were working faster. I was shocked that their speed increased. They were writing lots more stuff, in 4 colors, with a tremendous increase in speed and accuracy.

To help them trivialize the common kinds of errors, I began to name each kind of error. If you mis-copy the problem you have the "I mis-copied the problem syndrome". If you misread your own work you have the "I can't read my own writing disorder". The kids say these as they giggle. When I make one of the same errors on the board, they will call me on it. I'll say that I made another "*la boo boo*". They will laugh at me, and we'll go back to work.

Just how many problems can I make you do correctly in one day? I'm not sure, but we work till the bell rings, and our "*la boo boos*" are way down. Most days we were doing at least 25 problems in class.

By February that year we had completed all the topics in the Algebra 1 book. For the rest of the year I found an Algebra

2 book to use and we covered about half the topics in it, too. I never mentioned that I was using an Algebra 2 book.

The result was these low performers made tremendous progress. Their confidence was soaring. They were no longer convinced that they were not very good at math. All the evidence was to the contrary. Go figure. All that really happened was that they changed to a different process than they had used in the past.

Every time I think about that amazing year it makes me smile. I was blessed to watch about 60 students get past most of their issues with Algebra and like it. The time to experiment with slowing down their brains has made me a better teacher. I will most likely always remember that year as one of my favorites, because all the changes I was making were new to all of us and I was having fun playing with it. It was rewarding to see what was working, what wasn't working so well and figuring out what I was going to do next. What piece of Algebra do I want them to master next?

This is all Dr. Dan's fault, of course. As I sat as his feet taking all 3 levels of the NLP certifications and Maximum Performance Technology, he would always ask burning questions like, "How is it possible that they haven't already solved this problem in their life?", which was followed by, "What must be true in their model of the world that is causing the results we are seeing?" These questions too often go unanswered. They forced me to process what I am doing on a totally new level.

I ask myself those two questions everyday about each one of my students. The answers don't usually come easy, unless they do. Today, November 27, 2012, I asked a girl named Jade, if she had always been a genius in all her prior math classes. I was wondering if she had a confidence issue, as I was thinking I could see it on her face. The look on her face confirmed my suspicion. She is very brilliant, just not totally convinced, yet. Ever since she changed the organization of her work, her grades have been sky high and now she has a dilemma. Her dilemma is, how can she continue to believe she is not a genius in math when all her current work confirms that she is? I am fortunate to be the one watching her let her lack of confidence go. Her smile is all the evidence I need.

Isn't it amazing that just slowing down someone's brain could cause so many things to change? Who would have thunk it?

Affirmation: I am a genius and I apply my wisdom.

53

KIDS CHEATING ON THE FINAL EXAM

One year I caught 3 guys cheating on the spring final exam in Geometry. I had graded the A students paper first. Then when 2 guys who had lots of absences and failing grades made A's on the final, I suspected that they might have cheated. They also might have been innocent, of course.

I laid the two papers down beside each other and started looking for any irregularities. The work on the 2 papers was identical. It was arranged the same way. Each step was exact. They had copied someone's test. The A student sat close to them, so I compared his test paper with theirs. It was identical, too. He had let them copy his work. There was no doubt.

So what was I going to do about this little cheating episode? I wanted to settle the issue myself. So, I asked myself that burning question; "When the dust has all settled, what do I want the outcome to be?" I wanted 3 things.

1. They would all get a zero on the final exam.

2. They would have a chance to confess.

3. There would be no huge argument in a meeting with any of the parents.

I went looking for these guys. I found the first one in another class and asked if I could talk to him in the hallway. He would not confess. He said that when he finished the first page of the test he laid it on the floor and he doesn't have any idea if anybody looked at his paper as he was so busy finishing the test. The second one told exactly the same story. So did the A student. They had gotten their story straight.

I told the A student that I knew that he had let the other guys copy his test. He should confess what they had done. If he did not confess then he would be in a meeting with his mother, counselor, an assistant principal and me. I would lay out the three papers and the evidence would speak for itself. He cracked.

He said he had fallen into peer pressure. He knew he should not have done it. He was so sorry. Would I please not call his mother? I had already called all the parents. I had left a message at his house. Then he was concerned about his grade. What would his semester average be? The zero on the final made his A average drop to a 78. He asked if there was anything he could do, as he did not want to make a C. I said his grade would stay 78.

His mother called me at home that night. She had already confronted him about why I had called and left a message to call me. He had confessed to her as well. She was very apologetic. She said that he loved my class, that I was his favorite teacher and that he was so embarrassed. Her future concern was if the failure on the final would not make him eligible for football when school started in the fall. I told her he would be eligible.

I got what I wanted. I kept myself in charge of the process. Since one of the parents might call the office, I notified the assistant principal who would have been involved if things had gone up stream from me. I let him know that I had handled the situation, what I had done, that I had the proof they cheated and if he heard from any of the parents to let me know. He thanked me for taking care of it and said he would keep me posted. I never heard anything else about the cheating episode.

When all the dust has settled, what is an acceptable outcome? Ask yourself this question every time you are dealing with any problem. You'll be glad you did.

Affirmation: I am a genius and I apply my wisdom.

54

ALGEBRA 1 FAILURES ARE A BIG PROBLEM

Two times over the years the campus principal has called a meeting with the math department to fuss at us about too many failures in Algebra 1. They both asked questions like: What's the problem? Why aren't y'all teaching the curriculum? What do you plan to do about these failures? Do you ever check for understanding?

Well.

The first time it happened our principal wanted to hear from all of us so we went around the room and each of 12 teachers spoke. Our message was aligned. We wanted to hold the quality at a high level.

In those days we didn't have a credit plus lab for failing grades to be made up. If Algebra 1 was failed it had to be repeated the following year. Anyone who passed would be taking Geometry the next year. We were not willing to just pass students because they would not be ready to take on Geometry. Our principal turned beet red, yelled at us, slapped the desk and told us to water down the material and stormed out of the room. He wanted us to just pass them, regardless.

Whatever.

As a group we decided to not water down the material and to stay the course. In a way we dared him to fire our whole department. The kids that didn't pass the semester repeated Algebra 1 the next year.

The second time was in a different school. The principal called a meeting during the year we first opened a new high school. We only had freshman and sophomores so most all of us had a section or two of Algebra 1. The questions were much the same. What's the problem? Why aren't more passing? He really wanted us to just pass everyone. He wouldn't come right out and say that, so he danced around it? Again, he wanted a response as to why so many were not passing.

I took a deep breath and answered. I said that it was just the first grading period, that our students had come from 8th grade and some were ill prepared, but that the biggest issue was one of maturity, meaning a lack thereof.

The room was silent for what seemed like a long time, as we waited for him to respond. When he did he said something like: "Oh, they need to grow up some." He got it. Failing the first marking period could actually be helpful.

The failure rate the second marking period was half of the first. The decline continued as the students got the idea that they were not going to be passed along unless they put in the work.

Not to burst your bubble or anything, but many people new to our profession are shocked when they discover that it is their fault when students fail. Students that could not do the work have been passed along to such an extent that they eventually get out of high school and then find it very hard to pass college work. Not all are actually ready to take on college.

Around October of their freshman year in college when they get to the point where it is almost impossible to pass any or all of their classes, they wind up in the office of one of the Psychology professors. They are often advised to go home and work for a year or so and then come back. Their college might give them one more semester, or not. College work was too big of a jump for them as they were not prepared.

There are lots of great articles floating around from college Psychologists that prove this point. I can demonstrate it from statistics. In Texas around 25,000 students enter the

University of Texas and Texas A & M universities each year. Between 10% to 20% flunk out most years. These students were successful enough in high school to gain admittance, but did not do the work necessary to remain in college. Maybe they went crazy being away from home, couldn't manage their time and load, were irresponsible, drank too much, didn't fight off the temptation of drugs, skipped too many classes, were ill prepared to do college work and for whatever reasons didn't make the transition from high school to college.

All their hopes and dreams shattered. They were accepted into a prestigious college and were not doing well, depression set in and they are given the advice to go home and get a job.

Here's some suggestions to share with your students heading off to college.

1. Get a tutor even before a semester begins in all your most difficult classes.
2. Take all your classes in the mornings, if possible.
3. Eat lunch in the student union and go to the library each day.
4. Stay at the library until all your work that is due the next day is done. Then go play all night if you want to. Studying in the dorm can be very difficult. You need to be involved in all the goings on of college life. If your days' work is already done then you're good.
5. Write all your assignments in a planner, so you can see what is due each week for the entire semester.
6. Stay ahead of all deadlines for papers and projects.
7. Force yourself into any study group that you can. Show up and study with the group.
8. Consider smaller colleges. You will never be in an auditorium with 250 to 400 people taking the same lecture class. For me it was a blessing to attend a small college. I had access to all my professors who all knew

who I was. All of my classmates that were headed to professional schools were accepted. If you are good every professional school will want you. They will look at your grades and your professional school aptitude tests. You don't have to go to Harvard to become a doctor, just saying.

9. Make sure you have fun and get your work done. Do all your assignments and you will get the degree you seek.

10. Do your best to enter college with a few hours already passed. Take some AP courses or test out of some hours. Try to keep your college load between 12 and 15 hours for each semester.

11. Have the time of your life, I know I did.

Affirmation: I am a genius and I apply my wisdom.

55

YOU CAN'T MAKE ME GO TO THE OFFICE

Back in my early days of teaching, I was still learning classroom management. It was in the days where they still used corporal punishment at our school. The alternative school was born during that time to deal with unruly behaviors.

In one of my Geometry sections I had 2 seniors taking Geometry for the 3rd time. Their behavior was out of control. It was a daily issue. It was a struggle to keep them in check in a class of 35.

They got to where they took turns yawning, stretching their arms out as much as possible and grunting as loud as they could. They were showing off for sophomores daring me to do something about their unruly behavior.

One day one of them did his very loud yawn, pushing me over the edge, so to speak. I told him that I wanted him to get up and go to the office. He replied, "You are not big enough to make me go to the office. I'm not going anywhere and if you touch me I'm gonna kick your ___!"

I said, "So what you are telling me is that I cannot make you go to the office!"

He said, " _____(expletive deleted) right. It is impossible to make me go to the office!"

I said, "I think you are right!"

Then I looked at the student sitting across the aisle from him, told him to get up and go to the office, to run, not walk and bring back the Assistant Principal immediately. As the kid got up to leave, the guy cracked, and said he would go, got up and left.

I walked down to our math office, called the Assistant Principal, and told him that I did not care where he sent my problem child that I was not going to allow him back in my class. He did not say yes, but also did not say no.

About 30 minutes later, they showed up at my door. I was informed that the next time there was any trouble he would be transferred to a study hall for the balance of the year. He apologized only because he was forced to and came back into class.

I had asserted my authority and had been backed up by our Assistant Principal. Okay, I got what I wanted, although he would not be removed until he pulled something else, which he never did.

I went to lunch after class that day, feeling like I had handled the situation and got what I wanted in the end. The message had already been sent to the rest of my class that I was going to take care of unruly behavior. I really can make you go to the office.

After lunch I came back through the math office, the phone rang, I was called to the phone, and was met with an angry parent. It was the other mother of the other unruly senior student in the same class. His mother wanted to know what I had done to her son. I told her he had not been in class that day and that I had not seen him.

The Assistant Principal had found him during lunch and had given him the same ultimatum. One more event and he would be in study hall for the rest of the year. I did not have any more trouble with anyone in that class.

I have no idea how I thought so fast, to send another student to the office for an administrator, but it worked. (Now we have a button to push and there is a phone in our rooms.) I was not willing to let one of my students control my classroom.

Thirty-six years have passed, many things have changed with me and the system in which we work, but what has not changed is that I am in charge of my classroom and the students are not. I set my rules, post them on the wall, follow them consistently, call the parents first before writing a referral and have learned to handle all of my own problems.

Ask yourself when working on any classroom management issue, "When this is all over, what is an acceptable outcome that I can live with?" Then make that outcome happen, without ever calling the office.

Decades ago we would depend on the Assistant Principals to help us handle problems with student behavior. Even back then we wouldn't always get an outcome that was acceptable to us. So start at what you want the outcome to be and ask the parents to help you. I have found that most often, the parents will get on the same page and we will both insist the student's behavior changes.

I get what I want, as the student conforms, and asks me to please never contact their mother again. When they ask that, I know that the parents had my back. There is rarely any trouble afterwards.

Classroom management is always the biggest issue when people enter our profession. Make it a priority. Find the book "THE FIRST DAYS OF SCHOOL" and study it hard. Just remember, you are in control, the students are not, although they will test you. Set up all your policies and procedures, post them on your bulletin board and follow them consistently. You can do it.

Affirmation: I am a genius and I apply my wisdom.

56

DR. B FUSSES AT ME

One year I did not go to open house. It was on a Monday night. Several parents of my students were there. I put a sign on my door saying I would not be there. It really made Dr. B mad, so she fussed at me about it, both that year and the 2 years following, saying that I better never miss open house again.

I had a very good reason for not attending, which I had explained to her before and so a couple of years later when she fussed at me about it again I decided to 'clear the deck.'

I informed her that if the same situation happened again that I would not be coming to open house. She never mentioned it again.

Why did I miss open house? Glad you asked.

Some 30 years prior to my missing open house, our 2 oldest children went to Meadows Country School, which was only a kindergarten and first grade. It was a single room school, very small, and taught by Miss Jan. What a great experience for our kids! Miss Jan's son Josh became like one of our own. He was very close to both our son and daughter. We took him to Camp Blue Haven with us a time or two. We love Josh.

Josh had always wanted to go into the military, which he did. He loved being a soldier. On his last tour in Afghanistan he gave his life for the country he loved and in the process saved several members of his platoon.

His memorial service was on a Tuesday morning and was a 6 hour drive away. We left my school on the Monday of open house immediately after school let out. The memorial service was at 10 the next morning. There were over 800 chairs set up in an aircraft hangar on the base and the crowd was so large it was standing room only.

So after being repeatedly fussed at about missing open house one time. The next time she brought it up I told her that I had known Captain Meadows since the time he was in kindergarten. He was like one of my own. I baptized him into Christ at summer camp and that regardless of the timing of any event at our school that if one my kids was killed in war, or died any other way, I was going to their memorial service. If it happened to conflict with our open house I would not be there.

I was as respectful as I could possibly be. She said, "Well, we'll see about that"! She never mentioned it again.

I wish that I could tell you that all of our kids at school would outlive us. It has not been true for me as we lost several to car wrecks, war and disease. I loved them all. I know that you do, too. Hold them all close. God gave us the job of working with them to help them as much as possible and to love them all like our own, for a short but precious time.

Of course, you get a free pass to attend any memorial service, even if it means that you miss open house.

Affirmation: I am a genius and I apply my wisdom.

57

PRAYING FOR THE PRINCIPAL

My Principal did not like me or think I was any good, or so I thought. Hmm. I thought it dated back to before he was even the Principal at our school. I had his step son one year in my Geometry class. He came to talk to me one day towards the end of the school year and asked what his sons' Geometry grade was?

I said I had not taken any grades, as the grading period had only just begun, so there were no grades yet. It was during the first week of the last grading period. We had been prepping for the state exam that week and there were no regular grades at this point. He asked me again. I said, I did not know.

A year later he became our Principal. Then he became the supervisor of the math department. Then he kept asking me if I was going to retire. The message I was getting was that he was ready for me to be gone. Maybe I was just misreading things, or not?

At my end of the year conference with him, he asked if I was planning to retire. I said that I was not that I needed to keep going for a while. He asked me why. I said I had a 14-year gap in my teaching career and needed to keep going.

He asked me what I did during the 14 years. When I told him I had a degree in Bible and was a minister for 14 years. He seemed shocked. He did not know, he said. Then he began to talk about the Bible classes he had taken in undergrad. We had a nice discussion about Old Testament Survey. He seemed to be viewing me differently.

As the AP Stats program was growing, we were making new records for students getting college credit. He noticed and would mention it if we passed in the hall.

Every year I have a Stats seminar to help recruit students to take the class the following year. He came to the seminar one day in the lecture hall. We had 150 students in the lecture hall to hear two fantastic speakers, Dr. Simon Sheater, Department Chair of Statistics at Texas A & M and a local businessman who runs a billion dollar company. My Principal loved the presentation.

A year or so passed and I launched my video making of individual math problems. We hit about 40,000 views on 500 videos during that first year. My Principal began calling me Mr. YouTube.

During those dark days when I did not know what I could ever do to change my Principal's perception of me as a teacher and as a person I had begun to pray for him. The prayers were just for him, that God would bless him and help him through all the stresses that all Principals face. I never asked God to change my Principals perception of me.

God did that of his own accord. The truth is that I could never have changed my Principals perception of me, even if I had tried. I did pray that God would help me bloom where I was planted. He did.

Affirmation: I am a genius and I apply my wisdom.

58

TWO KINDS OF MATH TEACHERS

Our first math department chair when Stony Point High first opened was a very good leader. Opening a new school the first year takes a lot of extra work, so we all pitched in to get the school year started off with a bang. It was fun.

Mr. H was our first department chair. I learned a lot from him. One day he said in one of our math department meetings that there were only two kinds of math teachers.

1. A real math teacher.
2. Someone who gives calculator worksheets.

Ouch!

Which one am I?

I heard a girl say in class one day, "I don't have a real teacher, I have a coach"!

Ouch again, as I am an old basketball coach!

What is a real teacher anyway, according to us? What do our students think is a real teacher? How would our definition differ from our student's definition?

One of my colleagues says that maybe as many as half of our current faculty are not real teachers. They are apathetic, are not really passionate about their subject, don't follow almost any school policies, can't stand teenagers, are often mean and are just there to collect a paycheck. She thinks some of the administrators are the same way. Maybe she's right, maybe she isn't.

Ouch!

My definition of a real teacher would include the following:

1. They are passionate about their subject. It is impossible to hide! The students know if we are passionate about our subject, or not. They know if we actually know our subject, or not, too.

2. They love their students! Each student knows if you love them, or not. Try asking your students if any of their teachers hate them. They will start naming names.

3. If real teachers won the lottery today, they might decide to come back to work the next year, having hired an administrative assistant to keep up with their paperwork. They love their job! It could be hard to just walk away. They believe they would be giving up a big part of their life.

4. Real teachers notice when students are struggling and they act. They see when a kid meltdown is coming, get the student out in the hall, let them cool off and come back in when they are ready. Reading their students is easy and natural.

5. Real teachers have amnesia for all past student mistakes and conflicts. Every day when a class enters their room everyone has a clean slate.

6. Real teachers get more respect from their students because they give more respect.

7. Real teachers practice the golden rule. They treat all people the way they would want to be treated.

8. Real teachers are very good listeners. They would want students to go ahead and vent, to say anything they want or need to say. A real teacher's answers might be "Ok, I know that is how you feel." "Is it my turn to talk, yet?" "What else would you like to say?"

These ideas are just my perception of what comprises a real teacher. What would your definition be? Think back through all your high school teachers. Who had the greatest impact on your life? How did they do that? Why do you remember them? I bet it is not because of the subject they taught? What would your students say about you ?

Affirmation: I am a genius and I apply my wisdom.

59

KEVIN'S INTERSHIP

Kevin joined our faculty when we opened a big school in our district. His expertise was as a special education math teacher. His degree was in history. His math knowledge comes from working for a surveyor and is off the charts fantastic.

For the first 3 or 4 years he worked with us he was our main inclusion teacher. He helped me with Geometry 3 or 4 semesters, as well as spending 3 or 4 semesters with about 6 or 7 of our math teachers in Algebra 1 & 2 and Geometry. Up until this point, he had never taught a class by himself.

When they gave him a resource class the first time he hit the ground running and did a fantastic job. He has a genius level gift working with special education students.

He thinks he had the best possible internship that anyone has ever had because he saw many of us come at Algebra 1 & 2 and Geometry from different vantage points.

He says he teaches parallel lines like Massie, equation solving like Carter, proofs like Remec, graphing like Jones, etc.

He used whatever technique from each one of us that he knew helped the kids the most and became a composite of our entire department. After 3 or 4 years, he was an instructional expert in each class he taught.

He also stole freely from all of our classroom management styles. All teachers are unique. We have all discovered ways that we can make things work the way we want them to. Our ways are as varied as varied can be. There really is no other way.

Kevin's unique plan will most likely never be fully implemented in the public school system, as he believes that all new teachers should be assigned to spend a full semester with a half dozen experienced teachers in 3 courses for two years so they too develop their own unique teaching resources and strengths.

He says that if this ever happens so many young math teachers would not be continually leaving the teaching profession. He learned everything that he will ever need to do and how to deal with each and every possible scenario over the course of 2 or 3 school years, as well as becoming an expert in Geometry, Algebra 1 & 2.

I think that he is right. He had perhaps the best internship of anyone that has ever worked at our school. I do not know how, if ever, his plan could be put into action. Would time permit a local college to assign their prospective teachers to spend 2 class periods a day for 2 school years with different teachers, in different courses? Probably not, they have their own way of doing things. It might be helpful if at least one education professor at your local college actually ever taught in a high school. Just saying.

Kevin and whatever school he ever works for are the winners, of course.

There you go.

Affirmation: I am a genius and I apply my wisdom.

60

DON'T THINK ABOUT A CHRISTMAS TREE!

Holding a negative in unconsciousness is impossible.

Whatever you do, do not think about a Christmas tree! Wouldn't it be too late to stop, since your brain pulled one up to look at, didn't it?

Well, I tried to not think about a Christmas tree too, and I noticed that as I was typing the sentence about what NOT to think about I had a picture of one in my head, and you guessed it, it was a beautiful Christmas tree.

It was too late not to think about it, since I already had. And so had you, didn't you?

The mind is a video camera, a digital photo camera, and while it is recording all images, it does the same thing with the audio so there is not only sound to go with the photos and movies but your feelings as well. It also has a replay button, so the data can be accessed if you like and so that you can think about it or re-live it.

Where do you think the picture of the Christmas tree came from? It came from your mind's data file, right? Bring the picture back up and you can add a sound track of your favorite Christmas song.

If I told you that "Chestnuts roasting on an open fire" was my favorite phrase in a Christmas song, as soon as you knew it was my favorite, you could hear it as well, right, or not? Only if you could, of course. Nat King Cole is singing my version. Who is singing the track you can hear? James Taylor? Amy Grant? Or maybe Barbara Streisand?

So don't think about a Christmas tree, and while you're at it, don't hear "chestnuts roasting on an open fire". I meant the song, not the actual chestnuts roasting on the fire, as they are sizzling. The official title isn't The Christmas Song, isn't?

On the unconscious level, our unconscious mind cannot hold the negative because it will do what it just did and call up picture, sounds and feelings. It does it instantly and effortlessly. It was this fact that led to the invention of a hard drive in the first place, only the hard drive on your computer cannot hold very much data compared to your brain.

The one between your ears can hold so much data that to match it would take a hard drive the size of perhaps, a skyscraper. The Empire State Building for example, at night when it's all lit up. See it? It's orange, isn't?

So much power, with such amazing recall, and oh I almost forgot, the mind also has the power to make up whatever it wants, like a blue Christmas tree, or a pink one with purple bulbs on it, as well as a picture of what your car would look like if it was lime green with white polka dots all over it. A lime green, white polka dotted BMW, now, that looks funny, doesn't it?

Okay, I'll stop giving you pictures to make up, although you are doing it effortlessly and perfectly.

Now it's time for some applications.

I'm ready, if you are.

Here, we go.

Don't expect it to be too much fun.

It isn't unless it is, isn't it?

The painful part of what we have all done with our language is, at times we have sent the opposite message of what we intended to say to the unconscious hard drive of our students. We meant well. We meant what was right and good, but what might have happened with the words we used, was to unintentionally send the opposite message we intended onto their unconscious hard drive.

I'll start off easy, okay?

Here are two ways of saying the same thing. Fractions are horrible, I hate them, or, fractions are not fun and of all the things we do they are "the most not easiest." The second way of saying it feels better.

The last part of the sentence might make our English teachers blush, but surprisingly, as I tell my students that fractions aren't easy, I get no resistance from them. Unconsciously their minds record that fractions are easy, which is what I wanted them to think in the first place.

Instead of failure I say, not success.

Bad has turned into, not good.

Bored to death became, I'm not having fun.

Math being hard to do, changed to math is not easy to do.

For years, I said so many things that were not the right way to say them. I did not know, naturally, but after I did, I spoke differently. No one commented that my speech was strange, no student resisted the statement that fractions weren't always easy, but the more I told their unconscious minds that they were successful and that fractions were easy, the better they performed. Duh!

One of my friends from NLP Practitioner, likes to say the "not" drops out. She means unconsciously. It is very important to stop using negative words. Use some form of not, and the opposite of the negative word.

You will get less resistance from the students, while telling their unconscious minds that they can do it. If we knew how many things are recorded in their unconscious that are not serving them well and helping them, it could be shocking and we might be embarrassed, too.

So early each year in every class, since I know that the students don't really care for fractions very much, I will go on a run attempting to bombard them with the fact that fractions are easy. It goes something like this.

Raise your hand if you don't think fractions are easy. (hands raise.)

Nod your head if think that fractions are among the "most not easiest" of all math topics. (heads nod)

They just aren't easy, right?

We don't like them either, don't we?

Have you ever not liked fractions?

I thought you had not liked them sometimes, was I right?

So put your left hand on your math book and hold up your right hand and repeat after me the oath of fractions.

I swear or affirm, that fractions are not easy, and that I don't like them, and sometimes when I see one I might instantly think that, oh no, this will not be easy, so I have learned that before I decide that I am not going to get the right answer, I should at the very least wait to see if the fractions drop out of the problem, which would make me glad, and then of course without the not easy fractions there anymore, I can just relax. So help me God.

They consciously think that the oath of fractions is bizarre.

So do I, except I would probably say lame, and I do it each year because I want to talk to their unconscious minds and stop their fear of fractions.

If you teach math you have seen them look at a problem, see some fraction in it and immediately decide that they were going to not get the problem correct. Fraction phobia is real. All they have to do is see one to trigger it.

I have resolved to say fractions are not easy as many times as I can each year. The more times I say it, the more problems they get correct. So remember what I have already said many times, the unconscious mind is running the show, which is why it is so powerful to learn to talk to their unconscious minds, and the reason I decided to write this book anyway.

And, of course, don't expect your speech to change a lot, either, okay? And always remember that fractions are not easy.

Affirmation: I am a genius and I apply my wisdom.

61

TAG QUESTIONS

A TAG QUESTION is a add on to the end of a sentence, isn't it?

They can be used in a variety of ways, can't they?

They always elicit an unconscious response, as your mind will agree, or disagree, or answer the question however it wants to, doesn't it?

It isn't always fun, isn't it?

It shouldn't always be fun, shouldn't it?

You can play with tag questions if you want to, haven't you?

You can't unless you decide to, didn't you?

It seems strange to just add a tag question to the end of everything, doesn't it?

Only if it does, didn't it?

I'm noticing that all your tag questions include a contraction followed by the word it, don't they?

Oops, I ended that one in *they,* didn't I?

I suggest that using a contraction would be a good idea, isn't it?

It isn't actually required, isn't it?

I had a lot of fun with tag questions when I was taking all the levels of NLP training with Dr. Dan. His wife Linda said one day that I was stuck in tag question-ville. I supposed she was right, wasn't she?

She was.

Use tag questions to elicit unconscious agreement, can't you? You'll like using them, haven't you? won't you?

Affirmation: I am a genius and I apply my wisdom, didn't I?

62

THAT'S FUNNY RIGHT THERE!

Sometimes things happen at school that are very funny. Somebody says something that is hilarious and it will crack everybody up. When this happens in the general faculty meeting they tend to be priceless. Here we go with 3 hilarious things that happened in faculty meetings, all done by our resident Calculus teacher.

My former school was a class 6A high school in Texas. We had just under 3,000 students. Two hundred and fifty adults that worked there. So our faculty meetings could get boisterous.

During one faculty meeting an argument broke out as the Associate Principal was saying that we were no longer allowed to send students that were misbehaving in class out into the hall. We were told the students going up and down the hall were creating havoc and we could no longer say "go sit in the hall."

Miss B stood up and began to argue the point. What do you want me to do with them then, when I send them to the office nothing ever happens? Even so, she was told, she could no longer send the misbehaving kids into the hallway. She argued back, that she had a responsibility to the kids that were not misbehaving and could not keep the unruly kids in the room. "No", she was told, "no more misbehaving kids in the hall".

Back and forth it went and neither woman was willing to stop arguing. So, our Calculus teacher, who has a shield of the National Sarcasm Society on her Wall (it says at the bottom; Like We Need Your Support) decided to say something to Miss B to get her to stop. When she spoke her timing could not have been worse. It was one of those moments when the room goes totally silent for just a second and everyone in the room heard her comment loud and clear.

She said, "Miss B, don't you get it, just take the 29 kids who are behaving out in the hall and have class out there and leave the out of control student in the room."

It was so hilarious the faculty could not hold back the laughter. What began as a giggle, soon turned to uproarious laughter. The Associate Principal turned beet red and Miss B sat down. Our Calculus teacher got chewed out pretty good for that one and they put a nasty letter in her file.

That was funny right there.

The same Associate Principal said at the first in-service meeting the following year, in her opening comments, that our book study for the year would be the book GOOD TO GREAT. It was a great book, she said. It would help explain things like how an Algebra 2 student could fail the course but pass the state mandated Math Assessment Test the same year.

Our Calculus teacher raised her hand. The Associate Principal called on her and our Calculus Teacher said, "It is actually very easy to explain since there is no Algebra 2 on the State Math Assessment Test." Her comment got a huge laugh, again. She got written up again. They charged her with being right and logical in a faculty meeting. That's funny right there.

The third time was on the first day back at teacher in service when our principal said in his opening comments that there was not going to be one single sarcastic word spoken by any faculty member during the coming school year. Our calculus teacher leaned over towards the math department and said, "Massie won't be able to talk all year!" Of all the nerve, accusing me of being sarcastic. She owes me a poster from the National Sarcasm Society.

The proverb says *A cheerful heart is good medicine.* The first to say *"laughter is the best medicine"* was Henri de Mondeville in 1300 AD. Make sure you find a way to laugh at school.

Affirmation: I am a genius and I apply my wisdom.

63

PLAYING MUSIC IN CLASS

I learned this one from Dr. Dan, of course. I play music in class. I play an album from any group I like on long playing vinyl records. My turntable is part of an old timey looking radio box, that also plays cd's, cassettes, am/fm, and has a plug in for an ipod. It's new but looks like an old radio.

I most often use the music as a timer. Do these 3 problems during the next song. I turn it on and off a lot.

The other reason I play music is to displace some of the boredom of Algebra. The music livens things up. It helps create a warm comfortable atmosphere.

Whenever I play the soundtrack of "The Sound of Music", many of the students will sing or hum along.

I'll say corny stuff like, "the original title of this song was I HAVE CONFIDENCE IN ALGEBRA", instead of the song lyrics which are "I have confidence in confidence alone." It always gets a smile. They also like "The Devil Went Down to Algebra 2" instead of "The Devil Went Down To Georgia".

I believe if you smile more it's always a good thing. At times we teachers have bored the students to death. Liven things up for a change.

I play one of the cd's from 100 greatest classical songs on test days. I have played the same one for every test for the past 17 years. They never hear that music unless it is a test day. They get used to it. I turn it on and they take a dive deep down into their test taking mode. They get there faster as the music is anchored to test taking.

Check out Crosley Companies vintage radio box that plays everything, because you can't borrow mine. Lol.

The first new Crosley I had worked great until the cd player stopped working. I used it for 2 more years and just played records. I called Crosley during the summer to see if I could send it to them for repairs. They charged me $30 and I had to pay the shipping one way. They said if they couldn't fix it they would send me a brand new one. I got a brand new one. YEAH TEAM! I kept the empty box and Styrofoam packing so I can send it back if it stops working again.

You don't have to play music in class. I just play it to help create the atmosphere I want, to use as a timer and to anchor them to concentration on test days.

Create a healthy atmosphere for learning, however you can. Test out whatever scenario you come up with and have fun. Use music or don't use music, just use something to help them focus. You'll be glad you did.

Affirmation: I am a genius and I apply my wisdom.

64

CELINE DION'S DESK

I use humor for effect. I tell a joke every day. Like Rodney Dangerfield's jokes about how bad a cook his wife is. "At my house the foods so bad we pray after we eat". "I don't think meatloaf should glow in the dark", and "When I leave dental floss in the kitchen the roaches hang themselves."

I also use humor to help correct students who are off task. Celine Dion's desk is one example. She is the famous singer of Las Vegas and the movie *Titanic* fame. I use one of her songs to help correct off task behavior. As you may know, Celine is not a favorite of most high schoolers.

There is a sign with the words "CELINE DION WAS HERE" with an arrow pointing down to a chair in a corner of the room.

If someone gets off task during class I assign them to go sit in the corner in CELINE DION'S DESK. Then I play her song titled, "ALL BY MYSELF". Sometimes it gets hilarious. The 2nd song played is "WALK LIKE A MAN" by the Four Seasons for the guys, and "BIG GIRLS DON'T CRY" also by the Four Seasons for the girls.

Seldom do I send anyone to sit in Celine Dion's desk. When I need to, I do, and the whole room works harder. After two songs I let them go back to their regular desk. The sign stays. They know it is there and what it's for. Do you need to go sit in Celine Dion's desk? Most of the time the question is all that's required to get them back on task. Maybe the strangest thing is that the entire room will work harder, along with whoever is sitting in Celine's desk.

My point has been made, with humor that I want you to work during group work. They get the message. More work happens. Duh.

The real Celine Dion coming to my class some day and sitting in her desk is on my bucket list. It could happen! Ha! LOL

UPDATE: Last year on a review day during Algebra 2, everyone was quietly working on their video review and the music I was playing was a cd by various artists. "*All By Myself*" just happened to be on that cd and when it started playing one of the guys in the room got up, pulled his desk over under the "Celine Dion was here" sign and went back to work. It was funny! They giggled a bit and kept working. What a trip!

Affirmation: I am a genius and I apply my wisdom.

65

THE MANDARIN ORANGE ACT OF 2005

Pre-Calculus class was about to start one day when one of my students asked: "Mr. Massie, do you have a fork?" Really, I thought, a fork, when there is not supposed to be any food eating during class. The truth is our students have enough snack food in their backpacks to open an average size convenience store. Full boxes of cereal, extra-large bags of Doritos, apple sauce, cans of this, tins of that, mandarin oranges, too.

She wanted a fork so she could eat her can of mandarin oranges during my class. I didn't have a fork. She asked if she could eat the oranges with her fingers. I said her fingers should be eaten separately. Lol

Since I do not like students eating in class and since it is against the rules in the first place, I invented the Mandarin Orange Act of 2005. The title was a rip off from the 1978 movie *The In-Laws* with Peter Falk and Alan Arkin. The re-make of the movie is not nearly as good, just saying.

You can go to YouTube to find the clip around the dinner table where Peter Falk tells a hilarious story about some giant flies in the bush carrying off babies in their beaks. He says that they were protected by the Guacamole Act of 1917. It is hilarious!

So, I invented the Mandarin Orange Act of 2005. I made a poster size chart and hung it on the wall. The Mandarin Orange Act of 2005 only had 2 rules:

1. You may not eat food during class.
2. If you feel the urge to eat food, re-read rule #1.

The Mandarin Orange Act of 2005 is what Dr. Dan would call an *absurdity frame*. That's because it's totally absurd. I use *absurdity frames* a lot. One of my fellow NLP Master Practitioners said one day that I had become stuck in one long ongoing *absurdity frame*. They meant my whole life had become an *absurdity frame*. The truth hurts. Lol.

When we came back to school from the Christmas Holidays, my class said that they could now eat food in class, because the Mandarin Orange Act of 2005 had ended. I climbed up on a desk and changed the date on the poster to 2006. You know, I marked out the 5 and wrote a 6. They laughed.

Actually the absurdity frame corrected them with a smile. My evaluator asked about it too. My students also had accepted the unconscious fact, without any objections, I might add, that *eating food in class is absurd*.

Many thanks to Peter Falk and *The In-Laws*.

"What a guy"! And then there is "Serpentine Shell Serpentine"! (You might have to watch the 1978 version of the movie to understand.)

Affirmation: I am a genius and I apply my wisdom.

66

BIBBITY-BOBBIDI-BOO

One day during Pre-Calculus class my students were working during the last fifteen minutes of class on their assignment. A girl had a cd she wanted me to play. I said that I didn't ever play students music. She said it was Disney songs. I said that I would try one song, but would most likely turn it off after that.

We put the cd in and I pushed play. When the music intro began every head in the room came up. They all smiled and without prompting from me all sang, SALAGADOOLA MECHICKA BOOLA BIBBIDI-BOBBIDI-BOO.

I began laughing. What a crack up. They finished the singing of the entire song and then all went back to work.

I could have never planned anything so great. It also gave me the opportunity to mention that I never wanted to hear anyone say ever again that they couldn't remember something.

The next year I added some new used records I found at Goodwill to my collection of LP's. I found The Sound of Music soundtrack, as well as Camelot, My Fair Lady and Cinderella. I was also lucky to find soundtracks of Butch Cassidy and the Sundance Kid and The Sting. They sing along with most of the Sound of Music songs, too. (FYI: Used records at Goodwill are $.99 each, just saying.)

Makes we wonder how many opportunities we might have lost, to use things that the kids all know and can sing along with to some kind of advantage in the managing of our classrooms. Hmm. I wonder. Music seems to make math more fun for my students. Go figure. Today they all sang along with the Credence Clearwater Revival song, "Have You Ever Seen The Rain?"

WEEKEND UPDATE: Last Saturday at Upward Bound (A federal trio program for first generation future college kids) at Southwestern University I had a dozen students at the board working on a problem. I played the old Monkees song, "I'm A Believer", from YouTube, on my iPhone. I was surprised when they all began singing along. I told them I wasn't aware that they knew who the Monkees were. Actually they didn't, but said that they were just singing an Eddie Murphy song from SHREK. LOL.

Think about how you might use some music during your class, or not, and don't even ask if you can borrow my John Denver or Elton John record or my record player. I'll be using them every day.

Affirmation: I am a genius and I apply my wisdom.

67

THE DAY I DECIDED TO QUIT

On the last day of finals a few years ago, I decided that I would retire. I was very tired. It had been a long year. I told myself I had had enough. I would explain to my wife when I got home, but my mind was made up, I was going to call it quits.

The last exam ended at 1:15. All the students went home. I was finishing my grades. It was 3 pm. I was just about done. My plan was to pack up my room the next day, when no one was there. I was ready. I was sure.

Just before I was planning to leave, a young lady, Miss Millett, who took my AP Statistics class, came to say goodbye. She left me with a card. After I read her card, I knew that God was telling me not to quit. Oh boy. This proverb has always been true: "Man works the plans of his heart, but the Lord directs his steps."

Nine years have passed and I have not retired, yet. I framed the note from Miss Millett. It hangs on the wall behind my desk. I look at it many times each day, remembering the day I decided to quit. It was not time. God knew. I got the message. It was very clear. I am grateful.

In the past nine years, I have met many students and colleagues that I would have never known had I not kept going. The year following Miss Millett's departure, some *kid teachers* joined our math department.

I call them the *kid teachers* for a number of reasons. They are all in their 20's. They are just getting started in our profession. I am old enough to be their dad. I have friends who are in their 20's! Yes!

Hanging around with them has helped to keep me younger. Another kid teacher joined us last year. I first met her through the Upward Bound Program that I work in the summers. She came to UB during her 9th grade year. I have known her for 10 years. She is a brilliant mathematician and is off to a fast start in the teaching profession. Every time I see her, it makes me smile. I would have missed the opportunity to work at the same school with her, if I had quit.

Last summer, a week before we were to report for teacher in-service an email was sent out from our department chair, saying we were 3 math teachers short, so please suggest anybody you know who is certified. I suggested one name, a lady from our small group at church. I have known her family for about a decade. She applied and got the job. Her room is now across the hallway from mine. Small world, huh?

I was in college with one of the other kid teacher's dad, when we were both studying to be math teachers. My world around there kept getting more user friendly. Hmm, God kept sending people I had known in the past and the kid teachers to keep me going. Okay, there you go.

I do admit that I always pray that God will do whatever is best in my life, not what I always want, but whatever He knows is best for me. It was best for me to keep going.

It is easy to see looking back what God was doing. I'm thinking that I can go a few more years. After all, retirement is not even biblical. They all kept going. Moses kept going until he was 120. Sorry Moses, I will not be able to even tie your years of service record, as something tells me I will not teach for 52 more years. Still teaching at 120, now that's funny right there. Oops, now you can tell how old I am today.

Affirmation: I am a genius and I apply my wisdom.

68

UTOPIA FOUND

Once upon a time I heard a story about a graduate professor who assigned his class of graduate students a project to go out into the slums of Baltimore and find 100 boys in the 4th grade, make a profile of each boy and his family, and predict how they would turn out in 25 years.

They compiled a huge amount of data on these kids. Their conclusion was that about 85% of these boys would spend time in prison. They turned in their project and the professor placed it in his file cabinet.

Twenty-five years later the same professor took the old project out of his file and gave it to another group of graduate students. Their project was to find as many of these boys as they could and see what had happened to them after all these years. They were to interview them and make a detailed description of how their life had turned out.

They could only find about 80 of the boys. Only 4 had ever spent time in prison. The prediction was 85%. Oops! What was the explanation for that?

These kids were from poor families, lived in the midst of drug dealers and gangs and yet only 4 had ever been to prison. Why? So their interview questions changed. They wanted to know from the boy's perspective what had occurred to keep them on the straight and narrow.

They kept hearing the same teacher's name. She had had a tremendous influence on almost all these boys. What had she done that caused so much good to take place? She had changed the boy's lives. How?

They finally found her in a nursing home. Her mind was still sharp. They interviewed her for days trying to find out what she had done to save so many lives. She didn't really know what to tell them. They finally gave up! This lady holds a tremendous secret, can't tell us what it is, and it is obviously so powerful that it changed all these lives, we have exhausted ourselves searching and now, after all this, we have to walk away and never know her secret?

They were very dejected as they were leaving her room when they heard her say, "You know, I loved those boys!"

"No written word, no spoken plea
can teach our youth what they should be.
Nor all the books on all the shelves,
it's what the teachers are themselves"!
Anonymous, quoted by John Wooden

Affirmation: I am a genius and I apply my wisdom.

69

SALLY

I met Sally when I changed schools in year 3 of my teaching career. She was the calculus teacher at L. D. Bell High in Hurst, Texas. This was to be my first experience in a public school, as either a student or a teacher. I was about to enter a new and somewhat foreign world. I had a lot to learn.

Since I am a WHY person, I had many questions about how to handle all kinds of issues with the presenting of material and classroom management and just why teachers did things the way they did. I might have asked Sally a few hundred questions a week. I would explain a current situation and she would explain how she usually handled that kind of scenario.

During the years I taught at Bell it is impossible to even begin to describe how much I learned from her. That she would even be willing to give me a continual crash course in the greater world of teaching is something that I will always cherish.

She was a safe place to talk about anything and everything. As I would discover not everyone can be trusted. Having a safe place to ask questions, vent frustrations and gain shared wisdom was a major factor in my development as a teacher.

One of the most important things you can do as a teacher is to find a mentor like Sally. There is somebody that teaches at your school you need to adopt as your mentor, if you haven't already done so. You need someone who is trustworthy to lean on as you grow as a teacher. My suggestion is to find the smartest person in your department.

Avoid being afraid to go and ask something like, "I've got a situation and need to ask just how you have handled a similar situation." Or "I just had a wild conference with a parent and need your help!"

Happy hunting for whoever your Sally already is or who that person will be.

Affirmation: I am a genius and I apply my wisdom.

70

MESSENGER IN THE NIGHT

AUGUST 15, 2016 1:21 AM

Hi Mr Massie,

I know it's super late but I felt the urge to message you. I hope you remember me. I was in your first period AP Stats class.

I lost my cousin to a car accident. We watched his life slip away over the past 2 weeks. I remember you always mentioning in class how important family is, how family is irreplaceable and how at the end of the day they're all that matters.

I remembered this, I took off work for those 2 weeks and chose to indulge every second with him in the hospital. This is a lesson I'll carry with me the rest of my life. I think that's more valuable than any sort of theorem or formula from class.

Thank you

August 15, 2016 2:09am

So sorry for your loss! Good job taking off work! Cherish the memories. Yesterday was my older sister's birthday. She died in 1997. Thought about her all day.

Have been getting adjusted to working at Hyde Park High School. Class begins today at 8:25am. I'll be your advisor and friend for as long as I live. And since I'm open 24 hours a day, you can messenger me as often as you like. Proud of you.

August 15, 2016 2:15 am
Thank you, Mr. Massie. I appreciate that. Get some sleep!

August 15, 2016 2:20 am
I'll try! And of course I remembered you!

Affirmation: I am a genius and I apply my wisdom.

71

THE EVENING AT THE *"ROOST"*

July 27, 2011

"The Roost" is an outcropping of rocks on the side of the mountain just above Camp Blue Haven, outside Las Vegas, New Mexico. It has a beautiful view of the forest and two, ten thousand foot peaks, Hermit's Peak and El Cielo (The Sky) in the distance. It is a special place for many. Three nights during the summer camping sessions of Camp Blue Haven the Tuesday night evening worship is at *"The Roost"*. Last night was the last of the three for this summer. I was privileged to be able to go this year.

Camp Blue Haven became one of those special places for our family as our kids were growing up, as we worked on the 6th session teaching staff for 23 years. We all love Camp Blue Haven, as it is filled with so many great memories.

Our youngest son Neal died in 2006. One of his last requests was for us to take his ashes to *"The Roost"*. We granted his request and go as many times as we can each year and just hang out. Most times we are very peaceful there, sometimes we are not. We have to go and when we get there we will react however we react. It can't be predicted.

Last night there were 190 campers and about 100 adults at *"The Roost"* for the evening worship. It was great to hear the campers singing.

Since I can never tell how I will react at *"The Roost"*, I found a place way over on the left side so maybe I could hide, if need be. During the singing of "Shout Hallelujah", I lost it.

Tears were streaming down my face. At least no one could see me, right? Not.

I was caught by Misty Boyles and her daughter. Eddie and Misty Boyles are very good friends of ours from our Camp Blue Haven teaching days. Misty gave me a hug and they sat down. Her daughter saw me crying and it seemed to puzzle her.

I asked God to overwhelm me with peace, as only he can, and if it was okay, would He let Neal come stand beside me. I became very peaceful very soon. Crying one minute, calm the next. I had a sense that Neal was there.

The speaker stood and announced that his theme was *choosing*. It was a great talk. Of course, he said we should all *choose* to give our lives to the Lord. The topic had a different meaning to me, due to Neal *choosing* "*The Roost*" as his final resting place. Neal also *chose* "*The Roost*" as my final resting place. I agreed, of course.

As the lesson ended, a prayer was led. Misty's daughter held her hand up. She intended for me to hold it during the prayer. Her mother held up a hand as well. I obliged. The little girl said afterward that she wanted to hold my hand because she knew I missed my son. Jesus knew when he said that the Kingdom of God belongs to the little ones. They always get it.

At the conclusion of the worship at "*The Roost*", they have a tradition called the *silent walk*. The walk off the mountainside down into camp takes about 15 minutes. It always amazes me to witness 190 teenagers being *silent* on the trail. There is absolutely no talking.

Sometimes over the years, I have stayed behind at "*The Roost*", to enjoy the silence and the darkness of the forest and to reflect. Last night I was thinking about staying behind again, only to discover to my surprise, that I was ready to go.

I left there thinking about all my *choices* over the years, and what new *choices* I needed and wanted to make.

And just like always, it was good to go spend a little time at "*The Roost*" and remember.

72

EPILOGUE

My prayer for you is that you would choose, wisely. Choose your inner circle, wisely. Choose procedures for your classroom, wisely. Choose your words, wisely. Guard your heart, wisely. Be creative, laugh a lot and do whatever adds life to your class.

In closing, I'm thinking that I need to mention 2 things I pray for everyday as the day is unfolding. I found them in my Bible. The first is from *The Book of James* chapter 1. James says, "If any of you lacks wisdom, let him ask of God, who gives freely to all without finding fault." So pray for wisdom every day.

The second is from *The Book Of Luke* chapter 11 verse 13. "If you then though you are evil, know how to give good gifts to your children, how much more will your Father in heaven give the Holy Spirit to those who ask him!" So ask for the Holy Spirit.

His promise is that the answer to both requests for wisdom and to receive the Holy Spirit, is yes. It's His promise. So ask for wisdom and the Holy Spirit daily.

The Lord bless you and keep you, the Lord make His face to shine upon you and be gracious to you. The LORD turn his face toward you and give you peace. Amen.

Lloyd Massie Bio

Bachelor of Science in Education
Lubbock Christian University 1975
Secondary Math Certified Grades 6-12
Health/Physical Education Certified Grades 6-12

Bachelor of Biblical Studies
Abilene Christian University 1985

International Neuro Linguistic Programming Trainers
Association 1994-1999
Certifications in NLP Practitioner, NLP Master
Practitioner, NLP Business Trainer, NLP Maximum
Performance Technology, Time Line Therapy Practitioner
and Time Line Therapy Master Practitioner

34 Years Teaching Math in Texas Secondary Schools

10 years full time Ministry

www.ApplyYourWisdom.com

Facebook:ApplyYourWisdom

Twitter:ApplyYourWisdom